T.

A 52-week devotional to take you through the year and encourage you to see God in the ordinary

Allison T. Cain

Idea Consultant: Emma P. Cain
Editor: Adrianne Proctor
Cover Design: Kent Swecker
Family Photograph: Sara Grow

The LORD said, "Go out and stand on the mountain in the presence of the LORD, for the LORD is about to pass by."
Then a great and powerful wind tore the mountains apart and shattered the rocks before the LORD, but the LORD was not in the wind. After the wind there was an earthquake, but the LORD was not in the earthquake. After the earthquake came a fire, but the LORD was not in the fire.
And after the fire came a gentle whisper.

1 Kings 19:11-12

The Whisper of God for Kids

Published 2013. All rights reserved.

Unless otherwise noted, scripture quotations are from the *The Holy Bible, New International Version*, copyright 1973, 1978, 1984 by The International Bible Society.
Scripture taken from *The English Standard Version Study Bible*, Copyright 2008 Good News Publishers.
Scripture taken from THE MESSAGE. Copyright 1993, 1994, 1995, 1996, 2000, 2001, 2002. Used by permission of NavPress Publishing Group.

Allison Cain [atcain2@earthlink.net]
All Original Content Copyright 2013 Allison T. Cain

ISBN-978-1480159686
FIRST PRINTING

To order additional copies of this resource, visit
www.allisonTcain.com
For store locations, visit www.amazon.com
or e-mail atcain2@earthlink.net.

Printed in the United States of America

For my Emma and Culli, whom God uses daily to teach, encourage and convict me. I adore you both and I'm so grateful the Lord has entrusted you to us.

The Whisper of God for Kids

***

"Let us be silent, so that we may hear the whisper of God."
Ralph Waldo Emerson

Getting Started

As you go through the year, it is my prayer that you will discover two things.

1. God is at work in your everyday life. The more you get to know Him by studying the Bible and through talking to Him in prayer, the more you will sense Him at work in your life. He loves you so much that He is in every detail of your life at home, school and play.

2. Discover the value of reading the Bible. God wants to communicate with you, and He uses His Word (the Bible) to do so.

One more thing

This book has 52 devotions, one for each week of the year. Take your time. Read just one a week, sit on the scriptures in the devotion, think about them and reflect on them. Most of the verses will be short, but some will be a little longer and some will be repeated. Stick with it. I encourage you to use your Bible to look up your daily verses, but just in case you are somewhere without it, all the verses are in the back of your devotional. I pray God does some amazing things in your life and in your relationship with Him as you take this journey. Maybe your mom, dad or someone you are close to will go through *The Whisper of God* (for adults) so you can discuss what you are learning. You may even decide to get a small group of friends from school, church or your neighborhood together each week to share your thoughts and questions.

How to use this devotional

After each devotion, there is a section for you to write down your thoughts and questions. The format is simple. I call it the five W's.

Monday ~**W**rite~ Look up and write out the verse for the week. Write it in your book and on a note card you can put in your school notebook or on the bathroom mirror. Underline the words you don't understand and look them up or ask an adult what they mean.

Tuesday ~**W**hy~ Why do you think this verse is important for your life?

Wednesday ~**W**hat~ What can you do this week to show others what you learned from this verse?

Thursday ~**W**here~ Where did you see God in your week? Was a prayer answered? Did you feel peace during a test you were anxious about or find the courage to stand up for a friend being teased?

Friday ~Wow!~ Write down any other thoughts, questions or things you learned this week. Share them with a small-group leader, parent or other trusted adult.

∞∞∞

What's the deal with the anchor and the key?

We have this hope as an anchor
for the soul, firm and secure.
Hebrews 6:19

Each devotion will have an action item or a challenge for the week. You will see the anchor beside it. Write the challenge on your calendar or white board, or post it on your bulletin board for the week so you will be reminded to take the challenge. These actions will help you start living the words you read in the Bible and give you an anchor in Christ.

He will be the sure foundation for your times,
a rich store of salvation and wisdom and knowledge;
the fear of the LORD is the key to this treasure.
Isaiah 33:6

When you see the key, you will know that this week's devotion and work will be different. You will be practicing some methods to study God's word on your own and on a deeper level.

Week 1: God Doesn't Yell

Scripture: 1 Kings 19:11-12

We have a God who forgives, encourages, restores, loves, inspires and whispers. Yes, whispers! I am sure there have been days when my children wished I were more like God. No yelling! More whispering! Have you ever felt like that about your parents?

"Let us be silent that we may hear the whisper of God."
Ralph Waldo Emerson

Listen for God's whisper this week. He will guide you and help you make the right decisions.

I love this quote. I had it above the tub in our last house. What better place to be still and quiet, right?! It is such a great reminder of how God speaks to us. But we have to learn to slow down, reflect and listen to His whispers throughout the day – not just when we are in the bathtub.

God just wants to be your BFF. The One you go to for everything and lean on daily. He does not care where we have been, what we have done, how we acted in that situation with our friends … He accepts us for what we have been, washes us clean and restores us to who He created us to be – so we get to start all over. Oh, how I love our God!

Monday

Write ~ Look up and write out the verse for the week. Write it in your book and on a note card you can put in your school notebook or on the bathroom mirror. Underline the words you don't understand and look them up, or ask an adult what they mean.

_____

_____

_____

_____

_____

_____

_____

_____

_____

Tuesday

Why ~ Why do you think this verse is important for your life?

_____

_____

_____

_____

Wednesday

What ~ What can you do this week to show others what you learned from this verse?

_____

_____

_____

Thursday

Where ~ Where did you see God in your week?

_____

_____

_____

_____

_____

_____

_____

Friday

Wow! ~ Write down any other thoughts, questions or things
you learned this week.

_____

_____

_____

_____

_____

_____

_____

_____

_____

_____

_____

_____

_____

_____

Week 2: Pity Party
Scripture: Hebrews 6:12

I was having a bad day. I was hosting a pity party for myself. Everything seemed to be going wrong and I was feeling sorry for myself. I decided that I deserved this time to pout, and it was OK to have a pity party for myself as long as I didn't stay at the party for more than a few days. Have you ever had a time like that?

As we were driving down the road, my young son asked me, "Mommy, what are you going to be when you grow up. "Well, that is a great question," I told him, thinking if I don't know by now, I am probably in trouble. "How about Supergirl?" my son chimed in. "OK, sure. I will be Supergirl when I grow up." "OK, good" he said. "How about tomorrow?" "Tomorrow?" I asked. "Yes, why don't you grow up tomorrow?" he repeated. My son was right. It was time for me to grow up, take hold of God's Word and leave my pity party behind!

> Make a list of the people in your life that you look up to and lead Christian lives. These are people you can learn from.

I also began to think about how many times I had missed what God was trying to show or tell me because I was too busy, too distracted by my pity party. We need to take hold of God's promises and trust that our Father in Heaven is all we need, and He will provide and love us!

Monday

Write ~ Look up and write out the verse for the week. Write it in your book and on a note card you can put in your school notebook or on the bathroom mirror. Underline the words you don't understand and look them up or ask an adult what they mean.

_____

_____

_____

_____

_____

_____

_____

_____

_____

Tuesday

Why ~ Why do you think this verse is important for your life?

_____

_____

_____

_____

Wednesday

What ~ What can you do this week to show others what you learned from this verse?

_____

_____

_____

Thursday

Where ~ Where did you see God in your week?

_____

_____

_____

_____

_____

_____

_____

Friday

Wow! ~ Write down any other thoughts, questions or things
you learned this week.

_____

_____

_____

_____

_____

_____

_____

_____

_____

_____

_____

_____

_____

Week 3: Waters of Life

Scripture: Jeremiah 29:11

We had just spent the most amazing week in the North Carolina mountains. The cabin we stayed in was on 25 beautiful acres. Big Horse Creek ran right through the property. The sound of the water rushing through the rocks was mesmerizing. I would wade out to the center of the creek to sit on this huge rock. It was so big that it had created a fork in the creek, and water rushed by it on both sides. It is amazing how the years of water have molded, shaped and changed the rocks in the creek. They were all so unique in color, shape, texture and size.

I kept a rock from the creek to remind me of what God had taught me. What do you have (or can you find) to use as a visual reminder that God is with you?

It reminded me of how we all start out as one person and, as we go through the waters of life, we are molded and changed like the rocks. I have experienced so many joyful times, but I've also felt the sadness of losing a family member to cancer. There were times when the waters of life seemed like they might carry me away, but I've held firm in my trust of the Lord, even though I don't pretend to understand His plan! There are so many things that don't make sense to me, and I can't understand how they could be part of God's plan. I just remain faithful and know that God keeps all His promises and His plan is perfect.

Monday

Write ~ Look up and write out the verse for the week. Write it in your book and on a note card you can put in your school notebook or on the bathroom mirror. Underline the words you don't understand and look them up or ask an adult what they mean.

_____

_____

_____

_____

_____

_____

_____

_____

_____

_____

Tuesday

Why ~ Why do you think this verse is important for your life?

_____

_____

_____

_____

Wednesday

What ~ What can you do this week to show others what you learned from this verse?

_____

_____

_____

Thursday

Where ~ Where did you see God in your week?

_____

_____

_____

_____

_____

_____

_____

Friday

Wow! ~ Write down any other thoughts, questions or things you learned this week.

_____

_____

_____

_____

_____

_____

_____

_____

_____

_____

_____

_____

_____

Week 4: All the Money in the World

Scripture: Acts 26:18

It was just another day of running errands and trying to get everything checked off the to-do list. As we pulled into the parking lot of the bank, my son asked, "Mommy, where are we?" Before I could answer, my then-4-year-old daughter interrupted and said, "This is where we put all our money so we can save it to give to God to pay for our sins."

I giggled, but then I realized how scary that would be. I'm not sure how much money I would need to pay for my sins, but I am quite sure that we have nowhere near enough in our bank account! In fact, all the money in the world probably would not cover it! I stopped at that moment and said a prayer of thanksgiving. How grateful I am that God sent His only Son to die for me. How grateful and how astonished!

> ⚓ Do you have something you need to forgive yourself for? Pray to God for your heart to know and trust that you are forgiven.

No money, no kind deed, no donation, no gift nor speech is needed, just a confession of our sins to our Father in Heaven! It almost sounds too easy doesn't it? I think that is why it takes longer for us to forgive ourselves. Why we all feel guilt. It can stick around for days, weeks, months or even years. It is why some turn to shopping, gossip or other distractions. Sometimes it is difficult to trust that we are forgiven.

Monday

Write ~ Look up and write out the verse for the week. Write it in your book and on a note card you can put in your school notebook or on the bathroom mirror. Underline the words you don't understand and look them up or ask an adult what they mean.

_____

_____

_____

_____

_____

_____

_____

_____

_____

Tuesday

Why ~ Why do you think this verse is important for your life?

_____

_____

_____

_____

Wednesday

What ~ What can you do this week to show others what you learned from this verse?

_____

_____

_____

Thursday

Where ~ Where did you see God in your week?

_____

_____

_____

_____

_____

_____

_____

Friday

Wow! ~ Write down any other thoughts, questions or things you learned this week.

_____

_____

_____

_____

_____

_____

_____

_____

_____

_____

_____

_____

_____

_____

Week 5 ~ Forgiveness
Scripture: Micah 7:18

During a rushed Monday morning trying to get everyone out
the door, I lost my patience with the kids and yelled at them to
hurry up. Has your mom ever done that?

Later that morning, I asked my
son to crawl in my lap. As I
hugged him I told him I was
sorry I had lost my temper. I
explained that I was in a hurry
and frustrated, but I still should
not have yelled at him. He
hugged me and said, "I love it
when you say that, Mommy."
My son and I both finished the
day with smiles on our faces and happiness in our hearts.

> Have you done
> something to a friend
> or family member that
> you need to apologize
> for? This week, take
> the time to apologize.

What a powerful example that asking forgiveness and being
forgiven is such an important part of our lives. Can you
imagine the look on God's face when we ask Him for
forgiveness? Why is it so difficult for us to ask for forgiveness?
Why is it so difficult to forgive others after they have hurt us so
deeply? It is pride, disappointment, anger, bitterness?

I pray we all learn how to love more, forgive quickly and
extend grace freely like children do and our Father in Heaven
has and always will with perfection!

20

Monday

Write ~ Look up and write out the verse for the week. Write it in your book and on a note card you can put in your school notebook or on the bathroom mirror. Underline the words you don't understand and look them up or ask an adult what they mean.

_____

_____

_____

_____

_____

_____

_____

_____

_____

Tuesday

Why ~ Why do you think this verse is important for your life?

_____

_____

_____

_____

Wednesday

What ~ What can you do this week to show others what you learned from this verse?

_____

_____

_____

Thursday

Where ~ Where did you see God in your week?

_____

_____

_____

_____

_____

_____

_____

Friday

Wow! ~ Write down any other thoughts, questions or things
you learned this week.

_____

_____

_____

_____

_____

_____

_____

_____

_____

_____

_____

_____

_____

_____

Week 6 ~ May I Take Your Order?

Scripture: Isaiah 25:1

It had been a long morning, and I just wanted to go home and take a nap. I told my daughter on the way home from running errands that I would like to order a thunderstorm for the afternoon, because that would be great "nap-taking weather." She replied, "But Mommy, it's not a restaurant you can order from. It's God's thunderstorm. He will send it if He wants to."

I am certainly guilty of "placing my order" with God instead of prayerfully seeking Him, giving Him control and trusting in His perfect plan. I have learned the hard way more times than I would like to admit. Although I still make mistakes, I have become so much better at listening and learning from God. I have a strong desire to seek God's path for my life. I don't always understand it and I don't always like it, but when I trust in Him, He never lets me down and always provides me with more than I ever thought possible.

> Tell God that you are done placing your order with Him and you are ready for Him to lead you daily. Pray He will strengthen your trust and courage to follow His path.

It is so difficult to understand, but God has had a plan for you since before you were born. He knows you better than you know yourself. So when you need advice, answers and love, go to Him in prayer. His is listening to everything you think and say.

Monday

Write ~ Look up and write out the verse for the week. Write it in your book and on a note card you can put in your school notebook or on the bathroom mirror. Underline the words you don't understand and look them up or ask an adult what they mean.

_____

_____

_____

_____

_____

_____

_____

_____

_____

Tuesday

Why ~ Why do you think this verse is important for your life?

_____

_____

_____

_____

Wednesday

What ~ What can you do this week to show others what you learned from this verse?

_____

_____

_____

Thursday

Where ~ Where did you see God in your week?

_____

_____

_____

_____

_____

_____

_____

Friday

Wow! ~ Write down any other thoughts, questions or things
you learned this week.

_____

_____

_____

_____

_____

_____

_____

_____

_____

_____

_____

_____

_____

_____

Week 7 ~ GNATS!
Scriptures: Numbers 6:25-26

Yes, gnats! Those pesky little flies that love to hang around in the summertime. I was soaking in some morning sunshine and savoring a little quiet time for my Bible study. I was sitting right on the beach overlooking the water. The setting could not have been more perfect, except for the gnats! They were swarming around me. In my hair, my ears, my mouth. It was horrible! I knew this wasn't an accident. The Deceiver (Satan) would love nothing more than for me to stop studying God's Word. He will even use the smallest of insects to accomplish His goal. Well, I gave up on the perfect scenery and went inside, but kept studying!

What takes away your time from God? TV, texting, sports, friends? Take a break this week from that "worldly" thing and spend some more time with God this week.

I couldn't help but think of all the other little things in my life that distract me and keep me from studying God's Word, taking time to pray and listening for God's whisper. There are certainly more things to distract me from God than there are things that lead me closer to Him, especially in the world we live in. We need to get untangled and stop wasting our time on things of this world! We need to sort through the things that take up more time than God. We will always need God's help to stay focused on Him and not the things of this world.

Monday

Write ~ Look up and write out the verse for the week. Write it in your book and on a note card you can put in your school notebook or on the bathroom mirror. Underline the words you don't understand and look them up or ask an adult what they mean.

_____

_____

_____

_____

_____

_____

_____

_____

_____

Tuesday

Why ~ Why do you think this verse is important for your life?

_____

_____

_____

_____

Wednesday

What ~ What can you do this week to show others what you learned from this verse?

_____

_____

_____

Thursday

Where ~ Where did you see God in your week?

_____

_____

_____

_____

_____

_____

_____

Friday

Wow! ~ Write down any other thoughts, questions or things you learned this week.

_____

_____

_____

_____

_____

_____

_____

_____

_____

_____

_____

_____

_____

_____

Week 8 ~ "Saver"
Scripture: Psalm 25:5

It had been a tough day. As I was saying prayers with the kids before bed my eyes filled with tears. I had to pause for a moment to collect myself. My son looked up at me and wiped a tear off my cheek. He said, "Don't worry Mommy. I'll be your saver."

I wonder how many times my Father in Heaven whispered to me, "I'll be your SAVIOR," as He counted the tears that fell from my face, walked beside me during a time of sin or difficulty. I'm so thankful He never gave up on me and kept nudging my heart back to Him. He chased after my heart for many years before I was finally able to understand what it really meant to have Him in my life and accept all He was offering me. For so long, it was hard to comprehend how I could be worthy of His unconditional love, total forgiveness, grace, acceptance and mercy. The truth is, I'm not worthy of it!

> Is there someone you know that could use a Savior? Share Christ with them this week.

None of us are, but God gives it to us anyway. I thank God that He allows us to start fresh every day! Another chance to do the right thing, because there are many days when it feels I have failed miserably at pleasing Him. I praise Him for His amazing love, forgiveness and grace that never runs out or goes away.

Monday

Write ~ Look up and write out the verse for the week. Write it in your book and on a note card you can put in your school notebook or on the bathroom mirror. Underline the words you don't understand and look them up or ask an adult what they mean.

_____

_____

_____

_____

_____

_____

_____

_____

_____

Tuesday

Why ~ Why do you think this verse is important for your life?

_____

_____

_____

_____

Wednesday

What ~ What can you do this week to show others what you learned from this verse?

_____

_____

_____

Thursday

Where ~ Where did you see God in your week?

_____

_____

_____

_____

_____

_____

_____

Friday

Wow! ~ Write down any other thoughts, questions or things you learned this week.

_____

_____

_____

_____

_____

_____

_____

_____

_____

_____

_____

_____

_____

Week 9 ~ One More Thought: "Saver"

Scripture: Exodus 20:3

So many times I think we try to make a friend, teacher, parent or family member our "saver", instead of our one and only Savior, Jesus Christ. We are setting a course for disaster when we do this. There are three important things to remember.

Is there someone you go to for advice more than God? This week, practice taking everything to God first, and then to a trusted adult.

First, it is a sin to put any other before our Lord and Savior. It is the first of the Ten Commandments. It's even before those that say you shall not murder, steal or commit adultery. I believe if we would just follow this first commandment, all the others would never be a problem, because as we move closer to Christ, we desire to live more as He did.

Second, no one has the ability to give us unconditional love, grace, mercy and forgiveness; cleanse us of our sins; and promise us eternal life, except our Heavenly Father. He alone can give us those things.

Third, we are setting up ourselves and those we have placed in the "saver" role for a tremendous failure and disappointment. It can cause great hardship in the relationship and often end it.

Monday

Write ~ Look up and write out the verse for the week. Write it in your book and on a note card you can put in your school notebook or on the bathroom mirror. Underline the words you don't understand and look them up or ask an adult what they mean.

_____

_____

_____

_____

_____

_____

_____

_____

_____

Tuesday

Why ~ Why do you think this verse is important for your life?

_____

_____

_____

_____

Wednesday

What ~ What can you do this week to show others what you learned from this verse?

_____

_____

_____

Thursday

Where ~ Where did you see God in your week?

_____

_____

_____

_____

_____

_____

_____

Friday

Wow! ~ Write down any other thoughts, questions or things
you learned this week.

_____

_____

_____

_____

_____

_____

_____

_____

_____

_____

_____

_____

_____

Week 10 ~ She's Having a Moment

Scripture: James 1:5

We were at the mall one day before my daughter started kindergarten. It was time to eat and she wanted to choose the place. I was busy trying to explain to her that she got new earrings, so her brother got to choose where we would eat lunch. It didn't go well. As I crouched down in the middle of the mall trying to work through the tears and drama, some men passed by. I politely said, "Please excuse us. We are having a moment." My son speaks up and yells above the crying, "YEAH! She is having a moment." I wonder how many times God says that about me? "Oh, she is having a moment!"

This week, when you are "having a moment" stop and give it to God. Pray boldly and confidently and trust God to hear your prayers.

I often find myself caught up in "having a moment" about a situation, problem or concern, and realize that I haven't taken it to God. I have to remind myself to stop and go to God in prayer, seeking His wisdom, peace and guidance. I would love to be able to say I always realize this right away, but sometimes it's days before I remember to give it to God. Even if a request seems small or of little concern compared to a list of major prayer requests, be confident that He cares about every detail of our lives.

Monday

Write ~ Look up and write out the verse for the week. Write it in your book and on a note card you can put in your school notebook or on the bathroom mirror. Underline the words you don't understand and look them up or ask an adult what they mean.

_____

_____

_____

_____

_____

_____

_____

_____

_____

Tuesday

Why ~ Why do you think this verse is important for your life?

_____

_____

_____

_____

Wednesday

What ~ What can you do this week to show others what you learned from this verse?

_____

_____

_____

Thursday

Where ~ Where did you see God in your week?

_____

_____

_____

_____

_____

_____

_____

Friday

Wow! ~ Write down any other thoughts, questions or things you learned this week.

_____

_____

_____

_____

_____

_____

_____

_____

_____

_____

_____

_____

_____

Week 11 ~ Convicted

Scripture: Mark 8:36

In this selfish world we live in, there are many things to attract our attention away from God. If we don't take a time to study the Bible, pray and grow in our relationship with Him, we may gain the whole world but, as the scripture says, we will give up our soul.

I walked around for years calling myself a Christian, not realizing that I was not living like one. I made a lot of bad decisions during this time, and I'm sure my actions did NOTHING to bring others to know Christ. It took me many years to realize that what I had was religion, not a relationship. It is a relationship with Christ that makes us Christians. When that is in place, we can't help but start living in a way that is more pleasing to Him.

If you were arrested and convicted of being a Christ follower, would there be enough evidence to prove it?

Thank goodness God isn't looking for perfection, because I am far from perfect in my relationship with Him, but I am seeking Him in many ways through His Word and prayer that I know will change my life. I pray each day that I can live in a way that pleases God and will inspire others to come to know Him personally.

Monday

Write ~ Look up and write out the verse for the week. Write it in your book and on a note card you can put in your school notebook or on the bathroom mirror. Underline the words you don't understand and look them up or ask an adult what they mean.

_____

_____

_____

_____

_____

_____

_____

_____

_____

Tuesday

Why ~ Why do you think this verse is important for your life?

_____

_____

_____

_____

Wednesday

What ~ What can you do this week to show others what you learned from this verse?

_____

_____

_____

_____

Thursday

Where ~ Where did you see God in your week?

_____

_____

_____

_____

_____

_____

_____

Friday

Wow! ~ Write down any other thoughts, questions or things
you learned this week.

_____

_____

_____

_____

_____

_____

_____

_____

_____

_____

_____

_____

_____

Do not be <u>anxious</u> about anything, but in every situation, by prayer and <u>petition</u>, with thanksgiving, present your requests to God.[7] And the peace of God, which <u>transcends</u> all understanding, will <u>guard</u> your hearts and your minds in Christ Jesus.

Philippians 4:6–7 (NIV)

Use a dictionary and define the underlined words.

anxious

_____

_____

petition

_____

_____

transcend

_____

_____

guard

_____

_____

Now reread the verse and replace the words with the definitions you looked up. How did it give you a better meaning of the scripture?

_____

_____

_____

The Message translation is a Bible that puts Bible words into more common English language. Read *The Message* translation of today's verse below.

Don't fret or worry. Instead of worrying, pray. Let petitions and praises shape your worries into prayers, letting God know your concerns. Before you know it, a sense of God's wholeness, everything coming together for good, will come and settle you down. It's wonderful what happens when Christ displaces worry at the center of your life.

Philippians 4:6-7 (The Message)

Did you like this translation of the Bible? Did it help you understand the scripture even more than you did before? There are many different kinds of translations for the Bible. I like to study the English Standard Version (ESV), the New International Version (NIV) and The Message (MSG). There are Bibles that have the NIV and the MSG side by side, and there are also great websites, such as www.biblegateway.com that have all the translations. Try out some of these tools this week.

Week 13 ~ God Shows Off
Scripture: Matthew 6:34

There are not many times in my life that I can say God has responded instantly to a prayer. This isn't to say that He hasn't answered my prayers; He has answered many of them. He just doesn't always do it instantly! One summer night, I got one of those instant answers and it was amazing. I was sitting on our bed doing my Bible study and felt the need to pray for God to show me His presence. We do have a God who adores us and wants more than anything to have a love relationship with us.

So I simply prayed, "Father, thank You for Your abiding love and guidance. I pray that You will show me Your presence and show off for me. Lord, blow my mind." Not even two minutes later the fire alarm in our whole apartment building went off! We had to wake up the kids and evacuate. Thank goodness He just answered by fire alarm and not a real fire, but He did answer! The fire alarm has even more significance for me personally. Since I was a little girl, I have always been afraid of my home catching on fire. I would pack all of my purses with my favorite toys and leave them by my window so I could toss them out and climb after them if our house caught on fire.

Make a list of your fears and pray for God to take them from you.

I have found that the only answer to get rid of fear in my life is to give it over to my Lord and Savior.

Monday

Write ~ Look up and write out the verse for the week. Write it in your book and on a note card you can put in your school notebook or on the bathroom mirror. Underline the words you don't understand and look them up or ask an adult what they mean.

_____

_____

_____

_____

_____

_____

_____

_____

_____

Tuesday

Why ~ Why do you think this verse is important for your life?

_____

_____

_____

_____

Wednesday

What ~ What can you do this week to show others what you learned from this verse?

_____

_____

_____

Thursday

Where ~ Where did you see God in your week?

_____

_____

_____

_____

_____

_____

_____

Friday

Wow! ~ Write down any other thoughts, questions or things
you learned this week.

_____

_____

_____

_____

_____

_____

_____

_____

_____

_____

_____

_____

_____

Week 14 ~ Seek God First
Scripture: Psalm 63:1

Why do we take our problems, our concerns and complaints to others before we take them to God? He is the one we should go to first when we are seeking wise counsel. I had a lot of hard things going on. My friend was sick, my birthday was disappointing and I was feeling overwhelmed with all of my responsibilities. It was summer and all my friends were traveling, busy with camp, the pool, etc. When I tried to talk to them, everyone seemed distracted. They were out of town or running out the door to the next activity. Don't get me wrong, I am guilty of the same thing. We get in a hurry and fill our schedules to the brim so there is no time left for the things that pop up. After trying several times to talk to a friend and getting nowhere, it hit me! I realized I needed to be taking all of this worry and concern to God and trusting Him to be in control. I'm not saying we don't need to seek the counsel of our friends: God has placed them in our lives to support us, love on us, give us solid Christian advice and hold us accountable. I praise God for my friends every day! But God is never on the way out the door to swim-team practice, Target or the grocery store. We have a God who craves a relationship with us and desires for us to see Him.

> When a friend asks your advice this week ~ ask them if they have prayed about it yet and if they haven't, pray with them.

Monday

Write ~ Look up and write out the verse for the week. Write it in your book and on a note card you can put in your school notebook or on the bathroom mirror. Underline the words you don't understand and look them up or ask an adult what they mean.

_____

_____

_____

_____

_____

_____

_____

_____

_____

Tuesday

Why ~ Why do you think this verse is important for your life?

_____

_____

_____

_____

Wednesday

What ~ What can you do this week to show others what you learned from this verse?

_____

_____

_____

Thursday

Where ~ Where did you see God in your week?

_____

_____

_____

_____

_____

_____

_____

Friday

Wow! ~ Write down any other thoughts, questions or things
you learned this week.

_____

_____

_____

_____

_____

_____

_____

_____

_____

_____

_____

Week 15 ~ Listen & Obey

Scripture: Deuteronomy 5:27

Just this morning, I was reminding my children of how important it is for them to follow directions and do what I ask of them. Mid-sentence, I realized that this is what our Heavenly Father says to us each day as He speaks to us and we make the decision to listen and obey or move on with our own plan.

Hebrews 11 talks about faith and those in the Bible who demonstrated God-sized faith. This faith resulted in amazing and wonderful accomplishments – kingdoms were conquered, sinners turned to Christ, justice won and many escaped death. But faith also resulted in some terrible scenarios as it was used to torture, imprison, put to death and be cruel to Christians. The outcomes of faith are not always pretty! I know we all have the faith we need to follow God if we experience the good outcomes. The tough question is whether or not we have the faith to follow God when we endure the bad outcomes.

> Read Hebrews 11 this week and discover what God-sized faith looks like.

Do we have that much faith in our God? As Christians we can't just say that we have faith in God and His plan – we have to change our lives to reflect that we have faith in Him. If we don't step out and live like our God can do anything, why would others care to learn more about our God?

Monday

Write ~ Look up and write out the verse for the week. Write it in your book and on a note card you can put in your school notebook or on the bathroom mirror. Underline the words you don't understand and look them up or ask an adult what they mean.

_____

_____

_____

_____

_____

_____

_____

_____

_____

Tuesday

Why ~ Why do you think this verse is important for your life?

_____

_____

_____

_____

Wednesday

What ~ What can you do this week to show others what you learned from this verse?

_____

_____

_____

Thursday

Where ~ Where did you see God in your week?

_____

_____

_____

_____

_____

_____

_____

Friday

Wow! ~ Write down any other thoughts, questions or things
you learned this week.

_____

_____

_____

_____

_____

_____

_____

_____

_____

_____

_____

_____

_____

Week 16 ~ Victory

Scripture: Proverbs 19:21

I often try to tell God what I want to happen – how I want to do things and try to make Him change His plan to match mine.

Taking time to be still and know He is God is important, so that we are on track with His plan for us. God will make sure His plan is complete. The question is, do we want to jump in with faith and be a part of it, or do we want to sit on the sidelines because it wasn't how we thought it was going to be? If we have been taking the time to sit with God and develop that personal relationship with Him, it's much easier to trust, have faith and take action. He wants a conversation. He wants your trust and your confidence.

Pick one of the people mentioned today (David, Joshua or Gideon) and read their story.

There comes a point when we have to choose to believe that God is who He says He is and can do all things. There are many great stories in the Bible of those who trusted God, followed His plan and found victory. Look at David when he faced Goliath, **1 Samuel 17**. Joshua walked around Jericho waiting for the walls to fall, **Joshua 6**. Gideon sent almost all of his army home before the battle, and *won*, **Judges 7**. Unbelief is costly, but there is *victory* when we choose to throw away our plan and human wisdom and put our faith in God's power and His plan!

Monday

Write ~ Look up and write out the verse for the week. Write it in your book and on a note card you can put in your school notebook or on the bathroom mirror. Underline the words you don't understand and look them up or ask an adult what they mean.

_____

_____

_____

_____

_____

_____

_____

_____

Tuesday

Why ~ Why do you think this verse is important for your life?

_____

_____

_____

Wednesday

What ~ What can you do this week to show others what you learned from this verse?

_____

_____

_____

Thursday

Where ~ Where did you see God in your week?

_____

_____

_____

_____

_____

_____

_____

Friday

Wow! ~ Write down any other thoughts, questions or things
you learned this week.

_____

_____

_____

_____

_____

_____

_____

_____

_____

_____

_____

_____

_____

Week 17 ~ Wait
Scripture: Isaiah 40:31

Why is it so hard to wait on the Lord to answer our prayers? There are so many scriptures that tell us how important it is to "wait" on the Lord. One of my favorites is Isaiah 40:31.

I know that if I am waiting on anything, I feel like I am wasting time and that is one of my pet peeves, so it can be tough on me. However, I have found that waiting for God to speak is not a waste of time and takes hard work. It is a time to dig deeper, pray more and work towards a more intimate relationship with Him. It is not up to us to figure out the answers – all the responsibility is God's. We are trying to accomplish His outcome, not ours. Really, doesn't that just take a load off your shoulders? We don't have to figure it out. We just have to wait and respond in obedience.

Is there something you feel like you are waiting on? Waiting for the Lord to answer or show you? What lesson do you think God is trying to teach you while you wait?

We don't have to figure it all out on our own. More than anything, God wants us to be still, know Him, understand Him and wait for His whisper. I'm trying to appreciate the fact that "waiting" is taking me closer to God and taking me into a deeper relationship with Him.

Monday

Write ~ Look up and write out the verse for the week. Write it in your book and on a note card you can put in your school notebook or on the bathroom mirror. Underline the words you don't understand and look them up or ask an adult what they mean.

_____

_____

_____

_____

_____

_____

_____

_____

_____

Tuesday

Why ~ Why do you think this verse is important for your life?

_____

_____

_____

_____

Wednesday

What ~ What can you do this week to show others what you learned from this verse?

_____

_____

_____

Thursday

Where ~ Where did you see God in your week?

_____

_____

_____

_____

_____

_____

_____

Friday

Wow! ~ Write down any other thoughts, questions or things you learned this week.

_____

_____

_____

_____

_____

_____

_____

_____

_____

_____

_____

_____

_____

Week 18 ~ The Constant Battle

Scripture: Jude 1:24

"God wants us to beat up all the bad guys!" my son said with conviction. He was trying to convince my daughter of something she knew to be false, but he said it so boldly she stopped mid-conversation and had me confirm that his statement was false. I thought this was such a great example of how Satan works in our lives. We know our God! We know His promises! He never changes. He forgives. He loves. He is faithful and honest. The list of His great qualities goes on and on. However, when Satan starts to whisper in our ear we begin to question what we know of God and ourselves.

Satan can be so convincing that the things we are certain of one day, we distrust the next. We have to know our Heavenly Father inside and out and trust Him. When we know God intimately, we will be able to discern the truth and see through Satan's schemes. As soon as Satan anticipates a weakness or lack of faith on our end, he will begin to attack. Satan is real – just like God is. His lies, deceptions and sins swirl around us every day.

> Are you afraid, angry, or sad? Do you feel like you can't do anything right? That is Satan – not God! Turn your back on Satan, his lies and his betrayal.

The good news is our Savior sealed his fate. He is defeated! The only way Satan can affect us is if we choose to believe him over God.

Monday

Write ~ Look up and write out the verse for the week. Write it in your book and on a note card you can put in your school notebook or on the bathroom mirror. Underline the words you don't understand and look them up or ask an adult what they mean.

_____

_____

_____

_____

_____

_____

_____

_____

_____

Tuesday

Why ~ Why do you think this verse is important for your life?

_____

_____

_____

_____

Wednesday

What ~ What can you do this week to show others what you learned from this verse?

_____

_____

_____

Thursday

Where ~ Where did you see God in your week?

_____

_____

_____

_____

_____

_____

Friday

Wow! ~ Write down any other thoughts, questions or things you learned this week.

_____

_____

_____

_____

_____

_____

_____

_____

_____

_____

_____

_____

Week 19 ~ Eat What You Crave!?
Scripture: Romans 13:14

"Eat What You Crave." This was an actual advertisement on a billboard we passed while taking a family road trip. I was shocked when I saw it, but it made me think about some things.

These four words summed it all up. This is exactly the kind of world we live in. Our minds are filled with constant messages from the media, advertisements and Internet saying if it feels good, we should go for it. The world tries to tell us that if it feels good, do it – eat it, if you want it badly enough – do whatever it takes. In this self-absorbed world, there are more than enough pits to fall into, sins to overcome and temptations to resist. They are around every corner and in almost every situation we face. We were all born sinners, and when we are controlled by sinful nature, we can't please God. But we don't have to give in to sin. We need to choose God over sin. With Christ in the center of our lives, our thoughts and hearts can overcome our sinful nature. I am not saying this is easy. Let's face it: we wouldn't be so drawn to sin if it weren't fun. God doesn't give us rules, laws and commandments because He wants to control us. He knows how hurtful the results of sin can be to us and others. He wants to protect us from harm.

> Place a note on your bathroom mirror this week that says "Eyes on the Lord" for a reminder to keep your heart and mind focused on Him

Monday

Write ~ Look up and write out the verse for the week. Write it in your book and on a note card you can put in your school notebook or on the bathroom mirror. Underline the words you don't understand and look them up or ask an adult what they mean.

_____

_____

_____

_____

_____

_____

_____

_____

_____

Tuesday

Why ~ Why do you think this verse is important for your life?

_____

_____

_____

_____

Wednesday

What ~ What can you do this week to show others what you learned from this verse?

_____

_____

_____

Thursday

Where ~ Where did you see God in your week?

_____

_____

_____

_____

_____

_____

_____

Friday

Wow! ~ Write down any other thoughts, questions or things you learned this week.

_____

_____

_____

_____

_____

_____

_____

_____

_____

_____

_____

_____

_____

Week 20 ~ The Desert Place

Scripture: Psalm 136:16

A friend recently asked me to pray for her. She described her problem as being in a "dry" place, like a desert because she wasn't feeling close to God and wasn't sure how to get closer to him. Webster's Online Dictionary defines *desert* as: 1) arid land with usually sparse vegetation; an area of water apparently devoid of life 2) a wild uninhabited and uncultivated tract 3) a desolate or forbidding area. That definition certainly doesn't make you want to book an airline ticket and head off to the desert for your next vacation, does it?. As Christians, we can find these "desert times" stressful and scary. They can make us question our relationship with God and question God Himself.

I want to look at the desert in a different light and give it a new definition. If you search for scriptures throughout the book of Exodus, you notice that God called His people to "worship me in the desert" (Exodus 7:16); "journey into the desert to offer sacrifices to the Lord our God" (Exodus 3:18); and "hold a festival to me in the desert" (Exodus 5:1). So, let's redefine desert like this: 1) vast land that grows the bread of life; an area filled with the living water 2) a wild and exciting area full of opportunities to gain knowledge and grow closer with our Father in Heaven 3) an intimate and pleasant area. Now that's better!

> God speaks to us in four main ways: prayer, the Bible, the church and our circumstances. Are you listening?

Monday

Write ~ Look up and write out the verse for the week. Write it in your book and on a note card you can put in your school notebook or on the bathroom mirror. Underline the words you don't understand and look them up or ask an adult what they mean.

_____

_____

_____

_____

_____

_____

_____

_____

_____

Tuesday

Why ~ Why do you think this verse is important for your life?

_____

_____

_____

_____

Wednesday

What ~ What can you do this week to show others what you learned from this verse?

_____

_____

_____

_____

Thursday

Where ~ Where did you see God in your week?

_____

_____

_____

_____

_____

_____

_____

Friday

Wow! ~ Write down any other thoughts, questions or things
you learned this week.

_____

_____

_____

_____

_____

_____

_____

_____

_____

_____

_____

_____

_____

_____

Week 21 ~ Lift Up Your Hands
Scripture: Psalm 70:4

I saw a picture of a friend at an NC State basketball game. He was up in the stands with both arms raised, making the wolf sign with his fingers, wearing his NC State red and passionately cheering mouth-wide-open for his team.

It really made me stop and think. So many people attend rock concerts and sports games, raise their hands, cheer and worship the team, singers or players. Why can't people walk into church and feel like they can do the same thing?! It is certainly a good example of how our society elevates music, sports, self and Hollywood above all else, and sometimes we get sucked in. It is OK to join the crowds at sporting events or concerts in wild praise, but how about in church?

Have you danced with great abandon before God recently? Have you let your hair down and shown Him with praise how much He means to you and how thankful you are for His many blessings? Try it!

I am not going to tell you that I have always been comfortable worshipping with such emotion: hands in the air, eyes closed and soaking in the comforting and inspiring words of the music. However, as my relationship with God has grown more intimate, I am unable to keep from responding to His glory and majesty in a physical way.

Monday

Write ~ Look up and write out the verse for the week. Write it in your book and on a note card you can put in your school notebook or on the bathroom mirror. Underline the words you don't understand and look them up or ask an adult what they mean.

_____

_____

_____

_____

_____

_____

_____

_____

_____

Tuesday

Why ~ Why do you think this verse is important for your life?

_____

_____

_____

_____

Wednesday

What ~ What can you do this week to show others what you learned from this verse?

_____

_____

_____

Thursday

Where ~ Where did you see God in your week?

_____

_____

_____

_____

_____

_____

Friday

Wow! ~ Write down any other thoughts, questions or things
you learned this week.

_____

_____

_____

_____

_____

_____

_____

_____

_____

_____

_____

_____

_____

Scripture: Luke 12:48

A few years ago my husband gave me a bracelet for my birthday. It was silver with GODCHICK® engraved on it. I loved it, but eventually the bracelet wore out and I decided to make its message the personalized license plate on my car. I'll tell you, it can put a lot of pressure on a person when you're driving around town and everyone knows you're a Christian. No cutting people off or losing your temper. You get the picture! I have even thought to myself, "Maybe I should take it off." It is a lot of responsibility, and what if I can't live up to the example I need to set as a Christ follower? What if I need to scream at my kids one morning on the way to school because they won't stop arguing? Then I reconsidered and took a tough look at myself. Why does it take a license plate to make me feel like I should watch my actions? Instead, it should be that I want to please God and live in a way that brings others closer to Him. That is what so many Christians looked at as people who say one thing and do another. When we say one thing and do another it can cause others to turn away from Christianity. I don't want that person to be me. How about you? Even if we can fool others, we can never fool God.

> ⚓ Find a friend to hold you accountable to use kind words, do your Bible study or something else you feel like God is calling you to do.

Monday

Write ~ Look up and write out the verse for the week. Write it in your book and on a note card you can put in your school notebook or on the bathroom mirror. Underline the words you don't understand and look them up or ask an adult what they mean.

_____

_____

_____

_____

_____

_____

_____

_____

_____

Tuesday

Why ~ Why do you think this verse is important for your life?

_____

_____

_____

_____

Wednesday

What ~ What can you do this week to show others what you learned from this verse?

_____

_____

_____

Thursday

Where ~ Where did you see God in your week?

_____

_____

_____

_____

_____

_____

_____

Friday

Wow! ~ Write down any other thoughts, questions or things you learned this week.

_____

_____

_____

_____

_____

_____

_____

_____

_____

_____

_____

_____

_____

_____

Week 23 ~ Unconditional Love
Scripture: Isaiah 44:22

"Mommy, why do you always love me? Even when I do something wrong – you love me." I told him, "I always love you because I am your mom and you are my son." It wasn't a super explanation, but it's the simple truth.

That's how it is with God. We are His children, and when we have sinned or done something terrible we sit at His feet and say, "How can you still love me? How can you possibly forgive this?" His answer is so simple, it doesn't seem like enough. It feels like we should have to do more, pay a bigger price or suffer some sort of punishment. No! He forgives because He is our Father and His love for us is deep, constant and unconditional. If that love didn't exist, if He didn't love us as He says He does, there is no way He could have allowed His son to die on that cross for us.

Trust Him. Believe in Him. Follow Him. Celebrate Him. You are forgiven. God washes our sins away daily and allows us the opportunity to begin each day with a fresh start. Take advantage of it. Rejoice in it. Don't be a slave to sin. It will bring you down, harden your heart, make you lose your way, or lead you into more temptation.

> Forgive yourself for something you have done wrong and confess it to God. Trust in a clean slate and move forward!

Monday

Write ~ Look up and write out the verse for the week. Write it in your book and on a note card you can put in your school notebook or on the bathroom mirror. Underline the words you don't understand and look them up or ask an adult what they mean.

_____

_____

_____

_____

_____

_____

_____

_____

_____

Tuesday

Why ~ Why do you think this verse is important for your life?

_____

_____

_____

_____

Wednesday

What ~ What can you do this week to show others what you learned from this verse?

_____

_____

_____

Thursday

Where ~ Where did you see God in your week?

_____

_____

_____

_____

_____

_____

_____

Friday

Wow! ~ Write down any other thoughts, questions or things
you learned this week.

_____

_____

_____

_____

_____

_____

_____

_____

_____

_____

_____

_____

_____

All scripture is God-breathed and is useful for teaching, rebuking, correcting and training in righteousness.
2 Timothy 3:16

Use a dictionary & define the underlined words.

rebuke

_____

_____

training

_____

_____

righteousness

_____

_____

Now reread the verse and replace the words with the definitions you looked up. How did it give you a better meaning of the scripture?

_____

_____

_____

Use the space on the next page to write out the verse. The trick is … I want you to write it with your non-dominant hand. So, if you are right-handed, use your left; and if you are left-handed, use your right. It will slow you down and make you savor every word.

_____

_____

_____

_____

_____

_____

_____

Week 25 ~ Having Issues?
Scripture: Proverbs 3:5

On the way to preschool, my son said, "Mommy, I need to go to the doctor. I need some 'issues' medicine because I am having issues!" Oh, I got a wonderful laugh from his adorable statement, and I replied, "You know what? We all have issues, and some 'issues' medication would be great. I wish they made that." Of course, as my wheels started turning and I thought more about what he said, I heard the whisper: "It does exist. There has always been a medication for any issue you have. It is the Bible, God's written Word." Why isn't the Bible the *first* place we turn when we are faced with a problem or issue?

> Everything we need to know in order to live our lives to the fullest is in the Bible. God has provided the answers and direction. Open the Bible this week.

If we are sick we go to the doctor, if we need advice we call a friend, if we have trouble in math we call a tutor … the list goes on and on. What if our first stop was God and His Word? I wonder how many issues could be resolved by just stopping and having some quiet time with the Lord?

We can't do anything without the Lord by our side. Alone, our skills are completely useless, but with God anything is possible!

Monday

Write ~ Look up and write out the verse for the week. Write it in your book and on a note card you can put in your school notebook or on the bathroom mirror. Underline the words you don't understand and look them up or ask an adult what they mean.

_____

_____

_____

_____

_____

_____

_____

_____

_____

Tuesday

Why ~ Why do you think this verse is important for your life?

_____

_____

_____

_____

Wednesday

What ~ What can you do this week to show others what you learned from this verse?

_____

_____

_____

Thursday

Where ~ Where did you see God in your week?

_____

_____

_____

_____

_____

_____

Friday

Wow! ~ Write down any other thoughts, questions or things
you learned this week.

_____

_____

_____

_____

_____

_____

_____

_____

_____

_____

_____

_____

_____

Week 26 ~ Love vs. Fear

Scriptures: Zephaniah 3:17

I have been reading my son *Star Wars: The Clone War* books. He loves them and I confess I do too. I even enjoyed *Star Wars* as a child. Yoda is one of my favorite characters. "Yoda (the great *Star Wars* Jedi) said that fear is a way to the dark side of the Force." Even the little green guy gets it. Fear can destroy us, our faith, our trust and our focus on what is good and right. Fear can certainly lead us to the "dark side." Only, in our lives, the dark side is sin and Satan – not Darth Vader. What is the thing you fear most?

Look up these other verses that describe the awesome love that our God has for each one of us: John 15:9, Jeremiah 29:11 and Jeremiah 31:3.

The word love (loves, loved) is mentioned almost 700 times in the NIV. Have you ever tried to write a love letter or note to someone and express how much he or she means to you? Even for the best writer, it can be difficult to find words that express those deep emotions. For many, words aren't enough. We need to do something active for someone to express our love: visiting, mowing a yard, making a meal, sending a card, etc. Our God has done more than that for us. Not only did He leave us the descriptions and promises of His vast love for us in the Bible, He proved it when He allowed His son to die for us. Oh, He is all about LOVE. Love we can't even comprehend.

Monday

Write ~ Look up and write out the verse for the week. Write it in your book and on a note card you can put in your school notebook or on the bathroom mirror. Underline the words you don't understand and look them up or ask an adult what they mean.

_____

_____

_____

_____

_____

_____

_____

_____

_____

Tuesday

Why ~ Why do you think this verse is important for your life?

_____

_____

_____

_____

Wednesday

What ~ What can you do this week to show others what you learned from this verse?

_____

_____

_____

Thursday

Where ~ Where did you see God in your week?

_____

_____

_____

_____

_____

_____

_____

Friday

Wow! ~ Write down any other thoughts, questions or things you learned this week.

_____

_____

_____

_____

_____

_____

_____

_____

_____

_____

_____

_____

_____

Week 27 ~ Empty
Scripture: Proverbs 4:23

While we were waiting at the doctor's office, my daughter picked up a stethoscope, put the eartips in her ears and placed the chestpiece on her heart. She looked up at me with a smile and said, "Mommy, I hear God in my heart!"

Wouldn't it be nice if that were all we had to do to hear God working in our hearts? Especially the times when God seems to be silent and our hearts feel empty. I think we can be close to God, but our hearts can feel empty because of a circumstance we are dealing with, an answer we are waiting on from the Lord, a lesson we are learning, a broken promise, a lie from someone we have trusted, etc. As I looked up Bible passages that referenced the heart, I read that the heart can harden, weep, rejoice, crave, fail, soften, grieve (cry), hate, fear, praise, desire, despise, instruct, fight, love, discern (figure out), change, commit, seek ... and the list goes on. The heart can lead us down the right path if we guard it from emotions that eat away at its core and leave us feeling empty. However, I guarantee that if there is one spot in your heart that is not filled up by the Lord, Satan will find his way in with greed, anger, fear, guilt ... whatever will fit.

> Put on your stethoscope today and listen to your heart. Pray for God to reveal the weaknesses in your heart so that you can confront them, resolve them and clean them out.

Monday

Write ~ Look up and write out the verse for the week. Write it in your book and on a note card you can put in your school notebook or on the bathroom mirror. Underline the words you don't understand and look them up or ask an adult what they mean.

_____

_____

_____

_____

_____

_____

_____

_____

Tuesday

Why ~ Why do you think this verse is important for your life?

_____

_____

_____

_____

Wednesday

What ~ What can you do this week to show others what you learned from this verse?

_____

_____

_____

Thursday

Where ~ Where did you see God in your week?

_____

_____

_____

_____

_____

_____

_____

Friday

Wow! ~ Write down any other thoughts, questions or things you learned this week.

_____

_____

_____

_____

_____

_____

_____

_____

_____

_____

_____

_____

_____

Week 28 ~ Masks
Scripture: Ephesians 6:13

Masks! We have all worn them and most of us still do. Maybe not every day, maybe just around certain people or in certain circumstances. No, these are not the cute or scary masks we wear on Halloween or in a play. They're the ones we wear to cover up pain, shame, anger, fear or bitterness that has made a home in our hearts.

For years, I wore a mask of shame and guilt about past decisions I had made – decisions that had hurt others along the way. I had worn the mask so long I didn't remember how to take it off or even what I looked like underneath. After studying the Bible and learning who God really was, I was finally able to take off the mask. I didn't have to hide anymore. I found shelter under my Father's wing. I felt His forgiveness pour over me and realized how silly and wasteful it had been for me to wait all those years before accepting His forgiveness and shedding the mask. I don't think I had ever truly known God until that moment. It was a huge turning point in my life. After I threw away the mask I had been wearing all those years, I was able to put on the armor of God and He was able to start using me to share His good news. Satan no longer had a grip on me. I believed and knew God could use me to accomplish His will. Will you take that step today and take off your mask?

> What masks are you wearing? Practice taking your masks off this week and being yourself.

Monday

Write ~ Look up and write out the verse for the week. Write it in your book and on a note card you can put in your school notebook or on the bathroom mirror. Underline the words you don't understand and look them up or ask an adult what they mean.

_____

_____

_____

_____

_____

_____

_____

_____

_____

Tuesday

Why ~ Why do you think this verse is important for your life?

_____

_____

_____

_____

Wednesday

What ~ What can you do this week to show others what you learned from this verse?

_____

_____

_____

Thursday

Where ~ Where did you see God in your week?

_____

_____

_____

_____

_____

_____

_____

Friday

Wow! ~ Write down any other thoughts, questions or things
you learned this week.

_____

_____

_____

_____

_____

_____

_____

_____

_____

_____

_____

_____

_____

Week 29 ~ Please Pass the Salt
Scriptures: Colossians 4:5-6

"Mommy, you know that little boy who always calls me a baby at school? Well, I saw him today and he stuck his tongue out at me. He *DOES NOT* have God in his heart." My child's comment calmed my irritation and reminded me of what the appropriate response should be. "Well, I guess we better add him to our prayer list tonight and pray that God finds His way into his heart."

> Apologize to someone that you have hurt with your words this week.

I'll be honest: my tongue can be my greatest enemy if I am not careful. I have spent many days reading the book of James, because he has a lot to say about keeping your tongue under control. I have learned that **no man can tame the tongue. It is a restless evil, full of deadly poison. (James 3:8)** We have to rely on the strength and direction of our Lord to fill us with grace and His Word to season us so that our conversations and words are used to build up and not destroy. Words can hurt! Everyone has been the victim of a bad or angry tongue. Like a forest fire that starts out with a small spark, hurtful words can fuel a fire within us that leads to more evil and insults. Our job is to turn the evil or insult into a blessing. The dictionary says salt is used "to season, cure, preserve, or treat" certain things we eat or use. Let our Father in Heaven season you, cure you, preserve you and treat you through His scriptures so that your tongue does not overcome you.

Monday

Write ~ Look up and write out the verse for the week. Write it in your book and on a note card you can put in your school notebook or on the bathroom mirror. Underline the words you don't understand and look them up or ask an adult what they mean.

_____

_____

_____

_____

_____

_____

_____

_____

Tuesday

Why ~ Why do you think this verse is important for your life?

_____

_____

_____

_____

Wednesday

What ~ What can you do this week to show others what you learned from this verse?

_____

_____

_____

Thursday
Where ~ Where did you see God in your week?

_____

_____

_____

_____

_____

_____

_____

Friday
Wow! ~ Write down any other thoughts, questions or things you learned this week.

_____

_____

_____

_____

_____

_____

_____

_____

_____

_____

_____

_____

_____

Week 30 ~ Aliens Among Us

Scripture: 1 Peter 2:11

"Cross your fingers!" he said. "Oh, I'll do more than that," I explained. "I'll pray about it." Silence and an awkward laugh led the way to the next topic.

Sometimes I forget I am a foreigner in this world. I don't belong here. My real home (heaven) is in another place, with only a temporary address on this planet. I get the "look" more often than not. All I have to do is mention church, Bible study, prayer, etc. and there it is. It can be like telling someone you just got over the swine flu! They slowly back away.

Our hearts will always long for Heaven while we are here, but we have a loving God. I believe He offers us glimpses of eternal life and complete satisfaction. Wouldn't you agree that we get a little taste of Heaven when we see a beautiful sunset or receive a hug from someone we love?

God knew we would feel like we didn't belong here. This is not our home. Our place is with Him. Do you feel like an alien when you find peace in a stressful situation? Feel love where there was once anger or comfort where there should be pain? Do you pray instead of crossing your fingers? We may not have green skin or computer chips in our heads, but all these things can make us feel or seem foreign to others. Be proud of your foreign/heavenly heritage. Take comfort in knowing we will never be completely happy in this world.

Monday

Write ~ Look up and write out the verse for the week. Write it in your book and on a note card you can put in your school notebook or on the bathroom mirror. Underline the words you don't understand and look them up or ask an adult what they mean.

_____

_____

_____

_____

_____

_____

_____

_____

_____

Tuesday

Why ~ Why do you think this verse is important for your life?

_____

_____

_____

_____

Wednesday

What ~ What can you do this week to show others what you learned from this verse?

_____

_____

_____

Thursday

Where ~ Where did you see God in your week?

_____

_____

_____

_____

_____

_____

_____

Friday

Wow! ~ Write down any other thoughts, questions or things
you learned this week.

_____

_____

_____

_____

_____

_____

_____

_____

_____

_____

_____

_____

_____

Week 31 ~ The Bottom Line
Scripture: John 15:5

You know, God never changes. His lessons and messages have remained the same, and He keeps His promises. The bottom line is, the only thing that changes about God's Word is the people who teach or write about Him. Learning and studying the Word is so important. What are the ways you continue to fill your mind and heart with His Word? Is it Bible study, church, Sunday school, small group, blog, devotional, conversations with friends, or something else? All of these ways are great, but if you don't already take time alone with God and His word, I encourage you to do so. By listening only to others and not to Him, you are limiting what He can accomplish in and through you.

So today I urge you to sit down with God's Word and listen for His whisper as He leads and encourages you. Today, for just 30 minutes, choose God over your iPod, favorite television show or chatting on the phone.

Take a scripture and pore over it, soak it in, pray over it, absorb it into your soul, and ask God to reveal Himself to you. He will not let you down. When you are obedient and study His word, God is thrilled! He will bless you and show off for you in ways you never imagined. He will open your mind to things you never considered. When you serve God, you win!

Monday

Write ~ Look up and write out the verse for the week. Write it in your book and on a note card you can put in your school notebook or on the bathroom mirror. Underline the words you don't understand and look them up or ask an adult what they mean.

_____

_____

_____

_____

_____

_____

_____

_____

_____

Tuesday

Why ~ Why do you think this verse is important for your life?

_____

_____

_____

_____

Wednesday

What ~ What can you do this week to show others what you learned from this verse?

_____

_____

_____

Thursday

Where ~ Where did you see God in your week?

_____

_____

_____

_____

_____

_____

_____

Friday

Wow! ~ Write down any other thoughts, questions or things
you learned this week.

_____

_____

_____

_____

_____

_____

_____

_____

_____

_____

_____

_____

_____

_____

Week 32 ~ Infomercial

Scriptures: Genesis 4:6-7 (The Message)

My daughter came into the bathroom one morning to tell me all about a new cleaning product she had heard about on TV. "Mommy, you would love this. It cleans germs off the floor," she expressed with delight. Ten minutes later, she was back in the bathroom telling me about a new exercise program.

Like an infomercial, sin is waiting for us around every corner, just hoping we will have a weak moment, let our guard down and believe those lies inside our head: You aren't thin enough, you have earned it, you could do more, you aren't successful enough, they deserve it ... Satan can fill our heads with lies that we will begin to believe if we aren't filling up our hearts and minds with God's Word and truths. How do we master our sin? How do we seal up the cracks around our hearts and minds so that sin can't creep in and poison us? Fill your life with His Word, accept His blessings, praise Him in the storm, accept His direction, follow His path, allow His forgiveness to soak into your heart and share His love with others. Jesus has to be the guard for our heart!

> Why this tantrum? Why the sulking? If you do well, won't you be accepted? And if you don't do well, sin is lying in wait for you, ready to pounce; it's out to get you, you've got to master it. Genesis 4:6-7, The Message

Monday

Write ~ Look up and write out the verse for the week. Write it in your book and on a note card you can put in your school notebook or on the bathroom mirror. Underline the words you don't understand and look them up or ask an adult what they mean.

_____

_____

_____

_____

_____

_____

_____

_____

_____

Tuesday

Why ~ Why do you think this verse is important for your life?

_____

_____

_____

_____

Wednesday

What ~ What can you do this week to show others what you learned from this verse?

_____

_____

_____

Thursday

Where ~ Where did you see God in your week?

_____

_____

_____

_____

_____

_____

_____

Friday

Wow! ~ Write down any other thoughts, questions or things you learned this week.

_____

_____

_____

_____

_____

_____

_____

_____

_____

_____

_____

_____

_____

_____

Week 33 ~ Low Battery
Scriptures: Ecclesiastes 4:10-12

We used to have one of those battery-operated ride-on cars. The kids loved driving it around the yard and helping us do yard work, but when the battery starts to run low, it loses power and gets stuck much more often. I watched my two children ride together one day. If the car got stuck in the leaves or grass, my son would get out to push and my daughter would press the gas pedal until they were moving again and he could jump back in.

Do you know someone who could use a little help recharging? Are you in need of some recharging, but haven't been willing to accept the help? Seek God in prayer today.

It made me realize that as Christians our batteries sometimes run low. Our fire, hope, confidence and security in our Lord and Savior can lessen. We run low and forget the power and benefits of a full battery or a heart that runs completely with Christ. There are many reasons our battery can lose its charge: too busy to refuel, a challenging situation, sin or an unanswered prayer, and many more. Thank goodness we have friends, family, church members and strangers God places in our path, who can give us a push back to full speed. Sometimes it is difficult to accept help when we need it, and sometimes we think we are too busy to offer help to someone who needs it, but alone we can be defeated.

Monday

Write ~ Look up and write out the verse for the week. Write it in your book and on a note card you can put in your school notebook or on the bathroom mirror. Underline the words you don't understand and look them up or ask an adult what they mean.

_____

_____

_____

_____

_____

_____

_____

_____

Tuesday

Why ~ Why do you think this verse is important for your life?

_____

_____

_____

_____

Wednesday

What ~ What can you do this week to show others what you learned from this verse?

_____

_____

_____

Thursday

Where ~ Where did you see God in your week?

_____

_____

_____

_____

_____

_____

_____

Friday

Wow! ~ Write down any other thoughts, questions or things
you learned this week.

_____

_____

_____

_____

_____

_____

_____

_____

_____

_____

_____

_____

_____

Week 34 ~ Prayer
Scripture: 1 Peter 5:7

"Prayer is like that," she whispered, "Sometimes it can take days … months … years, and then sometimes when I get really quiet, I can see, hear and feel the answer all at the same time."

A very dear friend of mine gave me a gorgeous print with this quote. I absolutely love it! It sums it all up for me. There are times when I pray and get an instant response – and other prayers that seem to just sit out in space and take forever to be answered. The tricky part is learning to enjoy the wait and be thankful for all the blessings I already have.

Think of a time (maybe it is happening right now) when a family member was sick, you were having a hard time with friends or felt left out. How did you respond? You reached out, didn't you? And you wanted him or her to reach out to you, lean on you for help, support, love and advice.

Can you imagine being deeply content resting in God's shadow, trusting no matter what the situation, knowing He will provide you the strength to get through and that He is all you need? I think God allows needs to enter our lives so that we seek and depend on Him. It also gives Him the opportunity to show off for us and blow our minds with answered prayers we could have never imagined.

Monday

Write ~ Look up and write out the verse for the week. Write it in your book and on a note card you can put in your school notebook or on the bathroom mirror. Underline the words you don't understand and look them up or ask an adult what they mean.

_____

_____

_____

_____

_____

_____

_____

_____

_____

Tuesday

Why ~ Why do you think this verse is important for your life?

_____

_____

_____

_____

Wednesday

What ~ What can you do this week to show others what you learned from this verse?

_____

_____

_____

Thursday

Where ~ Where did you see God in your week?

_____

_____

_____

_____

_____

_____

_____

Friday

Wow! ~ Write down any other thoughts, questions or things you learned this week.

_____

_____

_____

_____

_____

_____

_____

_____

_____

_____

_____

_____

_____

_____

When my daughter was little, we lost her "meow" – the "meow" that helped her sleep at night. Oh, it was a rough few days until we finally discovered where we had left it. When we lose something we need or care about, we search high, low and in every drawer. We will retrace our steps, call every store we have visited and double back to check every stop we made. But what if we lose something forever? What if it's someone or something that can't be replaced: a pet, a parent or a dear friend? We still search high and low and retrace our steps, but we aren't looking for the person – we are searching for an answer.

> ⚓ Webster's Dictionary defines cling as: 1a) to hold together, 1b) to adhere as if glued firmly, 1c) to hold or hold on tightly or tenaciously, 2a) to have a strong emotional attachment or dependence. What do you cling to?

We are searching for an answer, someone to blame. For some reason, it makes us feel better or more in control if we can determine why or how something happened. We need answers. Finding joy can be a tall order. But we have a choice. We can shrivel up, hide, become bitter and overcome with guilt, or we can cling to our Lord and Savior. This is exactly what I mean when I say, "cling to our Father in Heaven." We have to glue ourselves to Him, emotionally attach ourselves to Him and not let go, because He will hold us up.

Monday

Write ~ Look up and write out the verse for the week. Write it in your book and on a note card you can put in your school notebook or on the bathroom mirror. Underline the words you don't understand and look them up or ask an adult what they mean.

_____

_____

_____

_____

_____

_____

_____

_____

_____

Tuesday

Why ~ Why do you think this verse is important for your life?

_____

_____

_____

_____

Wednesday

What ~ What can you do this week to show others what you learned from this verse?

_____

_____

_____

Thursday

Where ~ Where did you see God in your week?

_____

_____

_____

_____

_____

_____

_____

Friday

Wow! ~ Write down any other thoughts, questions or things
you learned this week.

_____

_____

_____

_____

_____

_____

_____

_____

_____

_____

_____

_____

_____

In Him we have <u>redemption</u> through His blood, the forgiveness of sins, in accordance with the riches of God's grace that He <u>lavished</u> on us with all wisdom and understanding.

Ephesians 1:5-8

Use a dictionary and define the underlined words.

redemption

_____

_____

lavished

_____

_____

Now reread the verse and replace the words with the definitions you looked up. How did it give you a better meaning of the scripture?

_____

_____

_____

Our children were invited to a friend's birthday party at the bowling alley. The attendant put bumpers in the gutters so the ball had no choice but to stay on the alleyway and hit a pin or two. She even set up a contraption that rolls the ball for you if it's too heavy to swing. The kids were guaranteed a smile and the opportunity to knock down a few pins every time.

Our lives are just like that alleyway. We try to stay on God's path – right down the center – but many times along the way we make a mistake or falter and end up in the gutter. I am just thankful that if we end up in the gutter with God we don't have to stay there to the end. When we repent (ask forgiveness), He will throw us back out there on the right path again. He forgives and forgets and He calls us to do the same. But how do we learn to stay out of the gutter? The more we fill up our gutters with God's Word, prayer and church, the less room there will be for us to fall into them.

And just like that special contraption that helps roll the ball down the alley, God is there for us when things get too heavy and we feel like we don't have the energy for one more day. He lifts us up, points us in the right direction and helps us get started, but we have to turn to Him.

Blessed be the Lord – day after day he carries us along. He's our Savior, our God, oh yes! He's God-for-us, he's God-who-saves-us. Lord God knows all death's ins and outs.

Psalm 68:19, The Message

Our God is for us – not against us! He is standing at the door of your heart waiting for you to allow Him in. Will you answer?

Here I am! I stand at the door and knock. If anyone hears my voice and opens the door, I will come in and eat with him, and he with me. Revelation 3:20

One of the greatest things we can do to grow in Christ is pray. In the space below write out a prayer to God. Confess your sins, thank God for His blessings and ask for God to direct your thoughts, actions and words.

_____

_____

_____

_____

_____

_____

_____

_____

_____

_____

_____

_____

_____

_____

_____

_____

_____

_____

Week 37 ~ Stuck in the Muck
Scripture: Psalm 40:2

The word "pit" is mentioned many times in the Bible. It can mean abyss, chasm, grave, tomb, well, hole, gorge – basically a REALLY deep hole. You get the picture. It doesn't really sound like a place we would choose to go, but sometimes we do. It is easy to fall into a pit of despair, self-pity, worry or fear.

I have been in a few "pits". In fact, sometimes I just tell my friends, "I am in a pit today, but don't try to get me out. I am down here and I just want to stay for a day or two. In a few days I promise to come out." We all get a good laugh out of it, but telling them where I am is important because they will hold me accountable and check in on me to ensure I make an exit.

You may not be in a pit, but do you know someone who is? Take some time this week to talk and pray with them.

Are you stuck in the muck? How long has it been? It may have only been a few days or it may have been for a while. Make a decision today. Don't put your time and energy in the "pit." Pray right now that your Father in Heaven will give you the strength and direction to pull yourself out. Tell a friend about your decision and ask him or her to check in on you to make sure you are staying on the right track.

Monday

Write ~ Look up and write out the verse for the week. Write it in your book and on a note card you can put in your school notebook or on the bathroom mirror. Underline the words you don't understand and look them up or ask an adult what they mean.

_____

_____

_____

_____

_____

_____

_____

_____

_____

Tuesday

Why ~ Why do you think this verse is important for your life?

_____

_____

_____

_____

Wednesday

What ~ What can you do this week to show others what you learned from this verse?

_____

_____

_____

Thursday

Where ~ Where did you see God in your week?

_____

_____

_____

_____

_____

_____

_____

Friday

Wow! ~ Write down any other thoughts, questions or things
you learned this week.

_____

_____

_____

_____

_____

_____

_____

_____

_____

_____

_____

_____

_____

Week 38 ~ Download Complete

Scriptures: Psalm 63:1

We live in a world of technology. We can upgrade to a new version of software, order food, books, toys, music or anything else our hearts desire without even leaving our home.

However, there are still a few things we can't get from the Internet. We can't stick our finger in the computer and download a relationship with God. We can't order one either. It takes effort, study and discipline to get to know Him.

We have to find the time to spend with our Lord and Savior. Without His direction we will wander through life missing out on His plan, His opportunities and the feeling of peace provided by His forgiveness.

Our Father in Heaven adores us! It's hard to imagine with the way we act and the things we do sometimes, but He does. He desires time with us and wants us to seek and enjoy time alone with Him. He wants us to get to know Him through His Word, prayer and quiet time so that He can grow us in ways we never imagined. The more we know Him, the more we trust Him, seek Him and are blessed by Him.

Take some extra time this week in your Bible. Go deeper. Look up a few of your favorite verses and read the entire chapter instead of just the verse.

Monday

Write ~ Look up and write out the verse for the week. Write it in your book and on a note card you can put in your school notebook or on the bathroom mirror. Underline the words you don't understand and look them up or ask an adult what they mean.

_____

_____

_____

_____

_____

_____

_____

_____

_____

Tuesday

Why ~ Why do you think this verse is important for your life?

_____

_____

_____

_____

Wednesday

What ~ What can you do this week to show others what you learned from this verse?

_____

_____

_____

Thursday

Where ~ Where did you see God in your week?

_____

_____

_____

_____

_____

_____

_____

Friday

Wow! ~ Write down any other thoughts, questions or things you learned this week.

_____

_____

_____

_____

_____

_____

_____

_____

_____

_____

_____

_____

_____

_____

Week 39 ~ Hideout
Scripture: Jude 1:20

"Where is your Dad?" I inquired. "Oh, he is working on his hideout," replied my daughter. It was true. My husband had spent several vacation days working on his new workshop. He was busy organizing, cleaning, designing and planning how he would hang his tools, store his equipment and organize everything efficiently to prevent clutter. Webster's Online Dictionary defines a hideout as "a place of refuge, retreat, or concealment." I picture a big tree house where you can hide away by yourself. I believe that as we continue to grow in our relationship with God, we should spend a little more time in our own "hideouts" planning, organizing and studying the Word of God.

> Do you have a place to hide out with God? A quiet place to get away from family and TV? If not, find a quiet place this week.

I often think about what Jesus did when He walked this earth. Surely, there is no better example for us to follow. Throughout the gospels we see examples of Jesus slipping away to "hide out" with God. When Jesus needed to recharge, receive direction, encouragement, strength or simply enjoy the presence of His Heavenly Father, He would simply slip away or find a quiet spot alone. Like Jesus, if we take some time to hide out with God, we can draw our strength, direction and peace from Him.

Monday

Write ~ Look up and write out the verse for the week. Write it in your book and on a note card you can put in your school notebook or on the bathroom mirror. Underline the words you don't understand and look them up or ask an adult what they mean.

_____

_____

_____

_____

_____

_____

_____

_____

_____

Tuesday

Why ~ Why do you think this verse is important for your life?

_____

_____

_____

_____

Wednesday

What ~ What can you do this week to show others what you learned from this verse?

_____

_____

_____

_____

Thursday

Where ~ Where did you see God in your week?

_____

_____

_____

_____

_____

_____

_____

Friday

Wow! ~ Write down any other thoughts, questions or things you learned this week.

_____

_____

_____

_____

_____

_____

_____

_____

_____

_____

_____

_____

Week 40 ~ Contentment
Scripture: Psalm 32:8

Our children were earning the privilege of opening an early Christmas present. It just so happened that our son was able to open his present a day before my daughter. She was so jealous. Not just about him getting to open the present early, but also about the gift he received. I heard it all – from "It's not fair!" "He gets everything and I never get anything!" – until she opened her own gift and saw what she had been given. Then, the roles reversed and my son was jealous while my daughter was rejoicing. What a mess! During my daughter's wait, I wanted to say so many things. "How can you say it isn't fair? You don't even know what you are getting! Just wait! Be patient, you will see your gift is just as great, if not greater!"

> Be thankful for who you are and what God has provided for you today. Find contentment in who you are at this moment, and find comfort in knowing that God is

I was reminded of how often we go through this same exercise with God. Have you ever asked, "Why them and not me? Why me and not them? God, have you forgotten about me? This isn't fair." While all along God is whispering, "Be patient and remain in Me, for I have rewards for you that you can't even imagine." The closer we are to God, the more our faith grows.

Monday

Write ~ Look up and write out the verse for the week. Write it in your book and on a note card you can put in your school notebook or on the bathroom mirror. Underline the words you don't understand and look them up or ask an adult what they mean.

_____

_____

_____

_____

_____

_____

_____

_____

_____

Tuesday

Why ~ Why do you think this verse is important for your life?

_____

_____

_____

_____

Wednesday

What ~ What can you do this week to show others what you learned from this verse?

_____

_____

_____

Thursday

Where ~ Where did you see God in your week?

_____

_____

_____

_____

_____

_____

_____

Friday

Wow! ~ Write down any other thoughts, questions or things you learned this week.

_____

_____

_____

_____

_____

_____

_____

_____

_____

_____

_____

_____

_____

_____

Week 41 ~ Just That Simple
Scripture: John 10:10

"Mommy, do you remember the Great Wolf Lodge?" my son asked. "Do you know why it is called that? Because it is GREAT, that's why!" he said.

Sometimes, it is just that simple. We don't need to over think, question or guess who our Lord and Savior is or what He promises. It is all in the name and written out for us in His Word. He is who He says He is. It is as simple as that if we will trust in Him.

Who is God? He is Truth, Light, Everlasting, Love, Deliverer, Rock, Gentle Whisper, Almighty, the Great I Am, Prince of Peace, Ancient of Days, Abba, Comforter, King of Kings, Teacher, Alpha & Omega, Counselor, Creator, Judge … I wish I had more room to continue. I encourage you to research more of the names of God in the Bible. It is interesting, encouraging and important to understand and remember who God is.

PRAY – Lord, we thank You for all that You are. Please cover us in Your Word and help us understand and believe that You are who You say You are. Amen.

Sometimes it really is that simple. We are loved and forgiven by Christ – no matter what. No special form, no fee … just ask and it's done!

Monday

Write ~ Look up and write out the verse for the week. Write it in your book and on a note card you can put in your school notebook or on the bathroom mirror. Underline the words you don't understand and look them up or ask an adult what they mean.

_____

_____

_____

_____

_____

_____

_____

_____

Tuesday

Why ~ Why do you think this verse is important for your life?

_____

_____

_____

_____

Wednesday

What ~ What can you do this week to show others what you learned from this verse?

_____

_____

_____

_____

Thursday

Where ~ Where did you see God in your week?

_____

_____

_____

_____

_____

_____

_____

Friday

Wow! ~ Write down any other thoughts, questions or things
you learned this week.

_____

_____

_____

_____

_____

_____

_____

_____

_____

_____

_____

_____

_____

Week 42 ~ No Coincidence
Scripture: Psalm 19:1

You may or may not have experienced it. A time when you heard a little voice in your head (or your heart) telling you to send a card to a friend, make a phone call, or just stop in to say hello to a friend, neighbor or church member. Or maybe it was a time when someone told you that God had placed you in their path, and you said exactly what they needed to hear. You were an angel or an answer to prayer. It wasn't a mistake. It wasn't your idea, but it WAS God. Thankfully, you were open and obedient to His nudge so that He could use you to touch the life of another one of His children.

Pay special attention to God's whispers and nudges this week. Allow Him to use you as His 'Plan A'. Be open to speaking that kind word or paying attention to those who need a listening ear.

There is nothing that brings you down to earth more than realizing the Creator of the Universe has stepped in and used you to touch the life of one of His children. I am fortunate to have been the recipient of such encounters. I have also been blessed with the opportunity of being used by God to reach out to someone who has sought Him and His presence in their life. I pray you will receive this message with an accepting heart, open eyes and responsive soul to the requests God is whispering to you.

Monday

Write ~ Look up and write out the verse for the week. Write it in your book and on a note card you can put in your school notebook or on the bathroom mirror. Underline the words you don't understand and look them up or ask an adult what they mean.

_____

_____

_____

_____

_____

_____

_____

_____

_____

Tuesday

Why ~ Why do you think this verse is important for your life?

_____

_____

_____

_____

Wednesday

What ~ What can you do this week to show others what you learned from this verse?

_____

_____

_____

Thursday

Where ~ Where did you see God in your week?

_____

_____

_____

_____

_____

_____

_____

Friday

Wow! ~ Write down any other thoughts, questions or things you learned this week.

_____

_____

_____

_____

_____

_____

_____

_____

_____

_____

_____

_____

_____

Week 43 ~ His Presence
Scriptures: Psalm 139:7-10

I can probably count on one hand the times in my life when I have truly felt the presence of the Lord. Emotionally, I feel His presence often, but physically it is very rare for me. One particular time stands out the most. When our daughter was 4 years old she had some medical issues arise. It all turned out fine, but it was a very difficult and scary time. I had gone out early one morning with our dog. I was enjoying a quiet moment when a gentle breeze swept up from behind and surrounded me. The breath of heaven blew in and wrapped around me. Tears began to well up in my eyes as I accepted this tremendous hug from the heavens. What an amazing reminder that God is with us in everything we do. Oh, how I wish I could experience this every day. His physical presence brought an overwhelming sense of peace, love, satisfaction and stillness to my soul. I look forward to the day He offers Himself to me again in this way. I pray that my heart, mind and soul stay ready to receive it.

Do you crave His presence in your life? What inspires His presence? Is it a song, prayer, a beautiful setting, meditation, reading His Word, taking a quiet walk or something else? Stop now and pray for God to reveal Himself to you in a way He never has.

Monday

Write ~ Look up and write out the verse for the week. Write it in your book and on a note card you can put in your school notebook or on the bathroom mirror. Underline the words you don't understand and look them up or ask an adult what they mean.

_____

_____

_____

_____

_____

_____

_____

_____

Tuesday

Why ~ Why do you think this verse is important for your life?

_____

_____

_____

_____

Wednesday

What ~ What can you do this week to show others what you learned from this verse?

_____

_____

_____

Thursday

Where ~ Where did you see God in your week?

_____

_____

_____

_____

_____

_____

_____

Friday

Wow! ~ Write down any other thoughts, questions or things you learned this week.

_____

_____

_____

_____

_____

_____

_____

_____

_____

_____

_____

_____

_____

Week 44 ~ All The Pieces
Scripture: 2 Samuel 7:28

When my dad lost his dog and his best friend we had been talking a lot about life, death, God and heaven – even more than usual. I was getting my son ready for bed that evening, and he said, "Mommy, I am going to give you all the pieces of my life." "Really?!" I said. "What should I do with them?" With confidence and trust he replied, "Whatever you want to."

Imagine if we were able to sit at the feet of our Lord and Savior and say, "Father, I give you all the pieces of my life."

> ⚓ Take time to reflect on what pieces of your life you are still holding onto. Is it your social life, school, work, family or some other challenge that you always have in the back of your mind?

Can we say that to Him and really mean it with all the faith and confidence in the world? We can't give Him just a piece; we have to trust Him with all the pieces.

Every time I think I have done this successfully, I find another piece of my life that I am holding onto and trying to navigate alone. When I find myself struggling to find peace or an answer, I pause and realize that I have not given it to God.

Locate it and hand it over today. Trust God to handle it. As my children say, "God knows everything!"

Monday

Write ~ Look up and write out the verse for the week. Write it in your book and on a note card you can put in your school notebook or on the bathroom mirror. Underline the words you don't understand and look them up or ask an adult what they mean.

_____

_____

_____

_____

_____

_____

_____

_____

_____

Tuesday

Why ~ Why do you think this verse is important for your life?

_____

_____

_____

_____

Wednesday

What ~ What can you do this week to show others what you learned from this verse?

_____

_____

_____

Thursday

Where ~ Where did you see God in your week?

_____

_____

_____

_____

_____

_____

_____

Friday

Wow! ~ Write down any other thoughts, questions or things
you learned this week.

_____

_____

_____

_____

_____

_____

_____

_____

_____

_____

_____

_____

_____

_____

Week 45 ~ Miles To Go
Scriptures: Deuteronomy 32:4

On a recent family trip we got the usual, "Are we there yet?" and "How much longer?" I think we use this approach when it comes to our relationship with God. We work toward a stronger relationship with Him but find we never complete the task. It can be discouraging. We find ourselves asking, "Are we there yet?" or "How much longer until I get it?"

A relationship with God is not a task we will ever be able to cross off our to-do list. It will not be completed in this lifetime, but we can't stop reaching for the goal, because we will grow stale. If we stop growing in Christ, our lives will become like a swamp where the muck and mud of life start to sink our spirit and clog our judgment, goals, direction and relationships. No matter where you are in your walk with God, you are not finished yet and have miles to go. Life is filled with obstacles and challenges. But, if we continue to build our lives on Christ and His blessed hope, we can resist the weight of this world. Don't give up on Him, don't stop studying His Word, and don't push Him out of your life when things seem tough.

> What are the areas in your walk with God that you feel like you need to focus on the most? Prayer, study, trust, faith, etc.

Monday

Write ~ Look up and write out the verse for the week. Write it in your book and on a note card you can put in your school notebook or on the bathroom mirror. Underline the words you don't understand and look them up or ask an adult what they mean.

_____

_____

_____

_____

_____

_____

_____

_____

_____

Tuesday

Why ~ Why do you think this verse is important for your life?

_____

_____

_____

_____

Wednesday

What ~ What can you do this week to show others what you learned from this verse?

_____

_____

_____

Thursday

Where ~ Where did you see God in your week?

_____

_____

_____

_____

_____

_____

_____

Friday

Wow! ~ Write down any other thoughts, questions or things
you learned this week.

_____

_____

_____

_____

_____

_____

_____

_____

_____

_____

_____

_____

_____

_____

Scripture: John 1:4

After His birth, you don't hear much about Jesus until He is 12 and travels to Jerusalem for the Feast of the Passover and gets lost (or so His parents thought). I wish there were more stories in the Bible about Jesus when He was a little boy. I have so many questions. After Jesus broke a dish or drew on the walls, did Mary always remember He was the Son of God and handle the moment with patience and grace? Did she ever forget He was God's son and raise her voice in frustration? Or was Jesus, even as a child, God's perfect son and never ran into a moment when He required discipline?

I wonder why God left out the stories of Jesus' childhood. I would love to know what kind of parents Mary and Joseph were. Certainly they would be the greatest of role models when it came to parenting. Do you think they yelled at Jesus when he drew on the walls or talked back or was Jesus the perfect child who always did everything right? Even though the Bible doesn't tell us, we can look to the Bible for examples of how to live and grow in wisdom and stature.

> Have you ever thought about what Jesus was like when He was growing up? What questions do you have?

Monday

Write ~ Look up and write out the verse for the week. Write it in your book and on a note card you can put in your school notebook or on the bathroom mirror. Underline the words you don't understand and look them up or ask an adult what they mean.

_____

_____

_____

_____

_____

_____

_____

_____

_____

Tuesday

Why ~ Why do you think this verse is important for your life?

_____

_____

_____

_____

Wednesday

What ~ What can you do this week to show others what you learned from this verse?

_____

_____

_____

Thursday

Where ~ Where did you see God in your week?

_____

_____

_____

_____

_____

_____

_____

Friday

Wow! ~ Write down any other thoughts, questions or things
you learned this week.

_____

_____

_____

_____

_____

_____

_____

_____

_____

_____

_____

_____

_____

_____

Scripture: Isaiah 44:24

"Is God the biggest person in the world?" my son asked. "Yes." I responded. "So, He is small enough to live in our hearts and big enough to hold the whole world?" he replied. I could not have said it better. Yes, our God is enough. He is full of enough love, forgiveness and grace to fill our hearts and our lives so that it will flow over into those around us. The One who created the heavens and the earth, who placed the stars in the sky and knows them by name loves you and me enough to live in us and to hold our cold, weary, misguided world in His hands. How I pray He never lets us go.

> Is there someone you look up to more than God? Turn this person over to God and ask Him to help you seek Him above all else?

Don't be fooled by idols of power, money, healing or pleasure. They are powerless (Isaiah 36:2), worthless (Psalm 31:6) and fragile (Isaiah 57:13), and will only bring shallow and temporary joy. Focus instead on the one and only God, our Father in Heaven who sent His son to live and die for us. He gave the ultimate sacrifice for you and for me. There should be no one above Him. We should praise His name and give thanks for His never-ending and undeserved grace.

Monday

Write ~ Look up and write out the verse for the week. Write it in your book and on a note card you can put in your school notebook or on the bathroom mirror. Underline the words you don't understand and look them up or ask an adult what they mean.

_____

_____

_____

_____

_____

_____

_____

_____

_____

Tuesday

Why ~ Why do you think this verse is important for your life?

_____

_____

_____

_____

Wednesday

What ~ What can you do this week to show others what you learned from this verse?

_____

_____

_____

Thursday

Where ~ Where did you see God in your week?

_____

_____

_____

_____

_____

_____

_____

Friday

Wow! ~ Write down any other thoughts, questions or things you learned this week.

_____

_____

_____

_____

_____

_____

_____

_____

_____

_____

_____

_____

_____

Week 48 ~ Treasures
Scriptures: Matthew 6:19-20

The gel in the ant farm quickly turned from a solid substance into a maze of turning and twisting tunnels and passages. The ants never seemed to sleep. They just moved quickly, climbing over one another and taking pieces of gel to the top only to descend into the tunnels again to continue their work. They worked night and day on creating their detailed habitat only to die in just a few months. Then the instructions said to simply rinse the dead ants out of the habitat and keep it as a 3D form of art.

> What if we started thinking past this moment and this life? What if we placed our focus on the big picture – the eternal picture? Can you imagine how the world would change?

Like the ants, I think that many of us get caught up in the "now." We put more energy into the "I wants" and the earthly treasures than we do the heavenly ones. Our world caters to this desire. We have drive-through food, downloadable books, music and movies, Internet shopping, stores on every corner; and if we don't have the cash, we can put it on the credit card. We collect and acquire things our whole life only to leave them behind when we die. Let's begin to focus on treasures that we can hold onto eternally and that can never be taken from us. For the things that we hold close and guard within our hearts can't be taken from us.

Monday

Write ~ Look up and write out the verse for the week. Write it in your book and on a note card you can put in your school notebook or on the bathroom mirror. Underline the words you don't understand and look them up or ask an adult what they mean.

_____

_____

_____

_____

_____

_____

_____

_____

_____

Tuesday

Why ~ Why do you think this verse is important for your life?

_____

_____

_____

_____

Wednesday

What ~ What can you do this week to show others what you learned from this verse?

_____

_____

_____

Thursday

Where ~ Where did you see God in your week?

_____

_____

_____

_____

_____

_____

_____

Friday

Wow! ~ Write down any other thoughts, questions or things you learned this week.

_____

_____

_____

_____

_____

_____

_____

_____

_____

_____

_____

_____

_____

Matthew 7:13-14 (ESV)

Enter by the narrow gate. For the gate is wide and the way is easy that leads to destruction, and those who enter by it are many. For the gate is narrow and the way is hard that leads to life, and those who find it are few.

The narrow gate is the way to Christ and the wide gate is the gate of the world.

What does the wide gate lead to? _____

Who enters it?   Few or many? _____

What does the narrow gate lead to? _____

Who enters it?   Few or many? _____

Matthew 7:21-27 – The Message Translation

21-23"Knowing the correct password—saying 'Master, Master,' for instance— isn't going to get you anywhere with me. What is required is serious obedience—doing what my Father wills. I can see it now—at the Final Judgment thousands strutting up to me and saying, 'Master, we preached the Message, we bashed the demons, our God-sponsored projects had everyone talking.' And do you know what I am going to say? 'You missed the boat. All you did was use me to make yourselves important. You don't impress me one bit. You're out of here.'

24-25"These words I speak to you are not incidental additions to your life, homeowner improvements to your standard of living. They are foundational words, words to build a life on. If you work these words into your life, you are like a smart carpenter who built his house on solid rock. Rain poured down, the river flooded, a tornado hit—but nothing moved that house. It was fixed to the rock.

26-27"But if you just use my words in Bible studies and don't work them into your life, you are like a stupid carpenter who built his house on the sandy beach. When a storm rolled in and the waves came up, it collapsed like a house of cards."

What will Jesus say if we haven't lived with God's word as our foundation? (Look at verse 23.)

_____
_____
_____

How does it make you feel to read that?

_____

Pray that God will guide you and help you be the smart carpenter whose house is fixed to the Rock [God].

Week 50 ~ Uncharted Waters
Scripture: Nehemiah 9:6

Recently, I found myself in a strange situation. Both of the strong, go-to people in my life were down. These are the two people I've always counted on to lift me up, keep things moving in a positive direction and just be there. They were both facing situations that were dragging them down and were barely able to keep their heads up.

I felt so helpless. Just able to sit, watch and pray. That never feels like enough, does it? In the tough situations, we usually want to take action and fix the problem! It has been a terrific reminder that I am not in control and that I AM NOT able to do it without God.

Make a list of all those people in your life that need prayer, and trust God to take care of them.

God is the qualified One. He alone. In fact, He does not even need our help. He may choose to get me to help Him in a certain situation, but He does not have to. He is Lord. Realizing this when you are watching those you love experience a confusing or painful time can be difficult. Let the following statements sink in as you read them. God is enough. Our faith and hope should be in Him alone! Prayer is enough! In fact, prayer is one of the most powerful tools God has given us.

Monday

Write ~ Look up and write out the verse for the week. Write it in your book and on a note card you can put in your school notebook or on the bathroom mirror. Underline the words you don't understand and look them up or ask an adult what they mean.

_____
_____
_____
_____
_____
_____
_____
_____
_____

Tuesday

Why ~ Why do you think this verse is important for your life?

_____
_____
_____
_____

Wednesday

What ~ What can you do this week to show others what you learned from this verse?

_____
_____
_____

Thursday

Where ~ Where did you see God in your week?

_____

_____

_____

_____

_____

_____

_____

Friday

Wow! ~ Write down any other thoughts, questions or things
you learned this week.

_____

_____

_____

_____

_____

_____

_____

_____

_____

_____

_____

_____

_____

Week 51 ~ Shine
Scripture: Ezekiel 1:28

You know those days or even weeks when you find yourself worn out from it all, the bad news has been more than the good and everything seems to be going wrong? As I was driving one morning, I was recounting (in my head) all the discouraging things that had been going on in my life and in the lives of those I love. As I topped a hill, I saw a rainbow in the sky. It was sunny with just a few clouds that were heading out after an overnight storm, but there was a rainbow. My thoughts immediately turned from sadness to praise and I felt peace overcome me.

God is our light on those dark days. He is the light that always shines in the darkness. Our God is so faithful and so tender. That rainbow was a beautiful reminder of His promises. Not just the promise that never again will the waters become a flood to destroy all life (Genesis 9:15), but a promise of His love for us. He is always with us. He walks with us through challenging times, He celebrates with us, He carries us when we can't take another step, He feels our pain and He counts our tears. The next time clouds overtake you, look to the sky. Look to God and rely on His promises to carry you through. He is there for you and His light never fades.

 Look up John 1:5 this week. What always shines through the darkness?

Monday

Write ~ Look up and write out the verse for the week. Write it in your book and on a note card you can put in your school notebook or on the bathroom mirror. Underline the words you don't understand and look them up or ask an adult what they mean.

_____

_____

_____

_____

_____

_____

_____

_____

_____

Tuesday

Why ~ Why do you think this verse is important for your life?

_____

_____

_____

_____

Wednesday

What ~ What can you do this week to show others what you learned from this verse?

_____

_____

_____

Thursday

Where ~ Where did you see God in your week?

_____

_____

_____

_____

_____

_____

_____

Friday

Wow! ~ Write down any other thoughts, questions or things you learned this week.

_____

_____

_____

_____

_____

_____

_____

_____

_____

_____

_____

_____

_____

Week 52 ~ Bold
Scripture: Luke 11:8

We had just had a long vacation from school. Everyone was having a difficult time getting back to our routine. We woke up on Tuesday morning running late, husband with a fever, kid's shoes muddy, and we barely made it to school before the last bell rang. Whew, I had dropped off one child and had one more to go before I could take a

> How can you be bold in your faith this week? Think BIG ~ think God!

breath. From the backseat I hear, "Mommy, let's talk about Jesus Christ our Savior." (I'm not kidding! That is a direct quote.) Talk about a jolt back to reality. It was like someone shaking me and saying, "Get it together, girl. Focus on what's important." My son's direct and very "in your face" statement was refreshing and clear. I wonder how many times we miss the opportunity to be bold and direct with those around us? How many times do we try to solve their problem(s) for them or offer our personal advice instead of pointing them in the direction of the ultimate solution – our Savior Jesus Christ. It isn't easy to be bold with those around us. Are we embarrassed? Feel like it is the easy way out? Do we not think He is a good enough solution, or do we just forget He cares? I think the answer varies depending on the day, the situation and the person with whom we are talking. Either way, try leaning on God more this week for the courage to take every opportunity He places in your path to share His good news and love with someone.

Monday

Write ~ Look up and write out the verse for the week. Write it in your book and on a note card you can put in your school notebook or on the bathroom mirror. Underline the words you don't understand and look them up or ask an adult what they mean.

_____

_____

_____

_____

_____

_____

_____

_____

_____

Tuesday

Why ~ Why do you think this verse is important for your life?

_____

_____

_____

_____

Wednesday

What ~ What can you do this week to show others what you learned from this verse?

_____

_____

_____

Thursday

Where ~ Where did you see God in your week?

_____

_____

_____

_____

_____

_____

_____

Friday

Wow! ~ Write down any other thoughts, questions or things you learned this week.

_____

_____

_____

_____

_____

_____

_____

_____

_____

_____

_____

_____

_____

Daily Scripture Reference

All scriptures are in order from week 1 through 52, and all are from the NIV translation unless otherwise noted.

1 Kings 19:11–12

The LORD said, "Go out and stand on the mountain in the presence of the LORD, for the LORD is about to pass by."

Then a great and powerful wind tore the mountains apart and shattered the rocks before the LORD, but the LORD was not in the wind. After the wind there was an earthquake, but the LORD was not in the earthquake.[12] After the earthquake came a fire, but the LORD was not in the fire. And after the fire came a gentle whisper.

Hebrews 6:12

We do not want you to become lazy, but to imitate those who through faith and patience inherit what has been promised.

Jeremiah 29:11

"For I know the plans I have for you," declares the LORD, "plans to prosper you and not to harm you, plans to give you hope and a future."

Acts 26:18

"… to open their eyes and turn them from darkness to light, and from the power of Satan to God, so that they may receive forgiveness of sins and a place among those who are sanctified by faith in me."

Micah 7:18

Who is a God like you, who pardons sin and forgives the transgression of the remnant of his inheritance?
You do not stay angry forever but delight to show mercy.

Isaiah 25:1

LORD, you are my God; I will exalt you and praise your name, for in perfect faithfulness you have done wonderful things, things planned long ago.

Numbers 6:25–26

"… the LORD make his face shine on you and be gracious to you;
[26] the LORD turn his face toward you and give you peace."'

Psalm 25:5

Guide me in your truth and teach me, for you are God my Savior, and my hope is in you all day long.

Exodus 20:3

You shall have no other gods before me.

James 1:5

If any of you lacks wisdom, you should ask God, who gives generously to all without finding fault, and it will be given to you.

Mark 8:36

What good is it for someone to gain the whole world, yet forfeit their soul?

Matthew 6:34

Therefore do not worry about tomorrow, for tomorrow will worry about itself. Each day has enough trouble of its own.

Psalm 63:1

You, God, are my God, earnestly I seek you; I thirst for you, my whole being longs for you, in a dry and parched land where there is no water.

Deuteronomy 5:27

Go near and listen to all that the LORD our God says. Then tell us whatever the LORD our God tells you. We will listen and obey.

Proverbs 19:21

Many are the plans in a person's heart, but it is the LORD's purpose that prevails.

Isaiah 40:31

… but those who hope in the LORD will renew their strength. They will soar on wings like eagles; they will run and not grow weary, they will walk and not be faint.

Jude 1:24

To him who is able to keep you from stumbling and to present you before his glorious presence without fault and with great joy—

Romans 13:14

Rather, clothe yourselves with the Lord Jesus Christ, and do not think about how to gratify the desires of the flesh.

Psalm 136:6

… to him who led his people through the wilderness;
His love endures forever.

Psalm 70:4

But may all who seek you rejoice and be glad in you;
may those who long for your saving help always say, "The LORD is great!"

Luke 12:48

But the one who does not know and does things deserving punishment will be beaten with few blows. From everyone who has been given much, much will be demanded; and from the one who has been entrusted with much, much more will be asked.

Isaiah 44:22

I have swept away your offenses like a cloud, your sins like the morning mist. Return to me, for I have redeemed you."

Proverbs 3:5

Trust in the LORD with all your heart and lean not on your own understanding;

Zephaniah 3:17

The LORD your God is with you, the Mighty Warrior who saves. He will take great delight in you; in his love he will no longer rebuke you, but will rejoice over you with singing."

Proverbs 4:23

Above all else, guard your heart, for everything you do flows from it.

Ephesians 6:13

Therefore put on the full armor of God, so that when the day of evil comes, you may be able to stand your ground, and after you have done everything, to stand.

Colossians 4:5-6

Be wise in the way you act toward outsiders; make the most of every opportunity. [6] Let your conversation be always full of grace, seasoned with salt, so that you may know how to answer everyone.

1 Peter 2:11

Dear friends, I urge you, as foreigners and exiles, to abstain from sinful desires, which wage war against your soul.

John 15:5 I am the vine; you are the branches. If you remain in me and I in you, you will bear much fruit; apart from me you can do nothing.

Genesis 4:6–7 (The Message)

GOD spoke to Cain: "Why this tantrum? Why the sulking? If you do well, won't you be accepted? And if you don't do well, sin is lying in wait for you, ready to pounce; it's out to get you, you've got to master it."

Ecclesiastes 4:10–12

If either of them falls down, one can help the other up. But pity anyone who falls and has no one to help them up. [11] Also, if two lie down together, they will keep warm. But how can one keep warm alone? [12] Though one may be overpowered, two can defend themselves. A cord of three strands is not quickly broken.

1 Peter 5:7

Cast all your anxiety on him because he cares for you.

James 1:2–4

Consider it pure joy, my brothers and sisters, whenever you face trials of many kinds, [3] because you know that the testing of your faith produces perseverance. [4] Let perseverance finish its work so that you may be mature and complete, not lacking anything.

Psalm 40:2

He lifted me out of the slimy pit, out of the mud and mire;
he set my feet on a rock and gave me a firm place to stand.

Psalm 63:1

You, God, are my God, earnestly I seek you;
I thirst for you, my whole being longs for you,
in a dry and parched land where there is no water.

Jude 1:20

But you, dear friends, by building yourselves up in your most
holy faith and praying in the Holy Spirit,

Psalm 32:8

I will instruct you and teach you in the way you should go;
I will counsel you with my loving eye on you.

John 10:10

The thief comes only to steal and kill and destroy; I have come
that they may have life, and have it to the full.

Psalm 19:1

The heavens declare the glory of God; the skies proclaim the
work of his hands.

Psalm 139:7-10

Where can I go from your Spirit?

  Where can I flee from your presence?

[8] If I go up to the heavens, you are there;

  if I make my bed in the depths, you are there.

[9] If I rise on the wings of the dawn,

  if I settle on the far side of the sea,

[10] even there your hand will guide me,

  your right hand will hold me fast.

2 Samuel 7:28

Sovereign LORD, you are God! Your covenant is trustworthy, and you have promised these good things to your servant.

Deuteronomy 32:4

He is the Rock, his works are perfect, and all his ways are just. A faithful God who does no wrong, upright and just is he.

John 1:4

In him was life, and that life was the light of all mankind.

Isaiah 44:24

"This is what the LORD says—your Redeemer, who formed you in the womb: I am the LORD, the Maker of all things, who stretches out the heavens, who spreads out the earth by myself,

Matthew 6:19-20

"Do not store up for yourselves treasures on earth, where moths and vermin destroy, and where thieves break in and steal. [20] But store up for yourselves treasures in heaven, where moths and vermin do not destroy, and where thieves do not break in and steal.

Nehemiah 9:6

You alone are the LORD. You made the heavens, even the highest heavens, and all their starry host, the earth and all that is on it, the seas and all that is in them. You give life to everything, and the multitudes of heaven worship you.

Ezekiel 1:28

Like the appearance of a rainbow in the clouds on a rainy day, so was the radiance around him. This was the appearance of the likeness of the glory of the LORD. When I saw it, I fell facedown, and I heard the voice of one speaking.

Luke 11:8

I tell you, even though he will not get up and give you the bread because of friendship, yet because of your shameless audacity he will surely get up and give you as much as you need.

~ ~ ~

Your journey doesn't have to end here.
With your parent's permission, you can visit my website at
www.allisonTcain.com

I update it regularly with new thoughts and lessons that the Lord is using to encourage and challenge me in my daily walk with Him.

***

I pray that out of his glorious riches he may strengthen you with power through his Spirit in your inner being, so that Christ may dwell in your hearts through faith. And I pray that you, being rooted and established in love, may have power, together with all the saints, to grasp how wide and long and high and deep is the love of Christ, and to know this love that surpasses knowledge – that you may be filled to the measure of all the fullness of God. Now to him who is able to do immeasurably more than all we ask or imagine, according to his power that is at work within us, to him be glory in the church and in Christ Jesus throughout all generations, forever and ever! Amen.

Ephesians 3:16–21

~Resources

www.biblegateway.com
www.biblestudytools.com
www.merriam-webster.com

Ken Anderson, *Where to Find it in the Bible,* (Nashville, TN:
Thomas Nelson, Inc., 1996).

Emma & Culli Cain, my sweet children.

Star Wars: The Clone Wars, Operation Huttlet, adapted by
Steele Tyler Filipek, based on the movie *Star Wars: The Clone
Wars,* 2008

~Many Thanks

I have so many things and so many people to be thankful for. My husband, children, parents and friends love, encouragement and support means more than I will ever be able to express. For that, I am more than grateful and so humbled.

Adrianne and Grover, my adopted family members, I can't thank you both enough for coming into my life. Your direction, leadership, advice, editing and training have shaped me into who I am as an author and speaker. I adore you both!

Emma Bean, first born, creative, nurturing little love bug. You are such a blessing to me. Thank you for all the reading time and thought you put into helping me make this happen.

Culli, my sweet handsome boy, thank you for playing basketball in the back yard so we could concentrate. I love you more than chocolate toast.

Mom & Daddy, the best parents in the WHOLE world, thank you for teaching me how to express love, seek God, persevere, encourage, motivate and forgive. You have both given me the most important gifts I will ever receive. I will treasure the memories we have made and the gifts you have given me in my heart forever.

77127645R00096

Made in the USA
Columbia, SC
22 September 2017